WE WANT OUR SAY
children as active participants
in their education

WE WANT OUR SAY
children as active participants in their education

Reva Klein

Trentham Books

Stoke on Trent, UK and Sterling, USA

Trentham Books Limited

Westview House	22883 Quicksilver Drive
734 London Road	Sterling
Oakhill	VA 20166-2012
Stoke on Trent	USA
Staffordshire	
England ST4 5NP	

First published 2003

British Library Cataloguing-in-Publication Data
A catalogue record for this book is available from the British Library

ISBN 1 85856 265 1

Designed and typeset by Trentham Print Design Ltd., Chester and printed in Great Britain by Cromwell Press Ltd., Wiltshire.

Contents

PREFACE

This book arose from conversations betweeen Leora Cruddas and Lynda Haddock who, at the time, both worked for Newham Education Department, and Nicky Road of Save the Children. We all three have a strong interest in having children's voices heard. Save the Children , as a children's rights organisation, has long campaigned for the right of children and young people to have a say in the decisions that affect their lives. In Newham one of the findings from a project exploring the social and emotional needs of girls was the girls' strongly held view that listening helps learning. In the words of one of the girls, 'If teachers listen to you then you will learn better because you feel good inside and then you can think better.'

All three of us felt that this was a good time to publish the arguments in favour of enshrining the right of children and young people to a voice in British law. There are positive signs that the government agrees that we need to engage young people in the vital decisions that will influence their futures. For example, the rights of children with special educational needs to be consulted about the provision that is made for them is set out in the new Special Educational Needs Code of Practice. All government departments have been asked to develop a strategy about consulting children and young people about the policies that shape their lives.

We asked Reva Klein, writer with a lively, accessible style who is able to combine solid fact with acute analysis to make the case for involving young people in the decisions that affect their lives. The resulting book offers an overview of the powerful arguments for children and young people's participation. It also gives inspiring examples of how teachers in schools have created communities where children and young people have their say and their views help to shape their learning. All children and young people have a right to speak out and be involved in real decision-making. This book describes both how this can be achieved and the real benefits for all those involved in education.

The book ends with a list of recommendations for schools and policy makers. We hope that when our readers finish this book they will be eager to make some of the changes we suggest and encourage young people to 'have their say'.

Leora Cruddas
Lynda Haddock
Nicky Road

CHAPTER 1
Creating democratic schools: the time is ripe

Student participation is in the ether and on the agenda. For the first time ever, legislation passed by Parliament has been put in place to ensure that children and young peoples' views are voiced, listened to and taken seriously in school. The Department for Education's guidance to schools on how to make themselves more democratic, interactive and accountable to students, hand in hand with Ofsted's new inspection remit to ensure that pupils are listened to, signals an exciting time for schools and a challenging one. These moves herald a potential shift in culture that brings children and young people into a power-sharing relationship with school managers, staff and governors.

The notion of democratising schools is based on the understanding that children's participation in how they learn and the environment in which they do so is a vital component of education in its wider, less measurable sense. Students who are involved in real decision-making, whose views are sought and listened to with respect, who interact constructively with teachers and their peers, are learning skills and ways of engaging with their community that are indivisible from the more standard realms of learning. School effectiveness therefore is as much about raising pupils to be proactive, adaptable, socially and emotionally intelligent and questioning participants in their education and in the wider world as it is about improving attainment.

This book will be discussing school reforms that are no longer in the wilderness of 'experimentation' but are in use in this country and elsewhere and are being promoted by statutory and non-statutory bodies in the UK. Giving students the role of active stakeholders in their own education and in the running of their schools is not only government policy but is in harmony with the principles and spirit of education for citizenship, the underpinnings of the Children's and Young People's Unit at the Department for Education and Science and, in the wider sense, the UN Convention on the Rights of the Child and the Human Rights Act.

The approaches that are discussed in these pages are exciting and of their time. Some are radical but are tried and tested, such as creating structures that enable primary as well as secondary schoolchildren to be represented on governing bodies or sit on interview panels for new staff, or give feedback on the quality of teaching they receive, or mentor and educate their peers. All have far-reaching benefits. When developed and implemented thoughtfully and rigorously, they can raise students' self-esteem, behaviour and attainment and improve teachers' job satisfaction. It is not overstating the case to say that they have the power to enhance the very ethos of schools and impact on the interactions of staff and students. Neither is it overstating it to say that such approaches are adaptable to all schools, from those in the greenest and leafiest of suburbs to those in areas of high social exclusion.

The changing landscape

It is also not overstating things to say that the philosophical goalposts of schools have changed beyond recognition in the last couple of decades. Public accountability – to parents, to Ofsted, to education authorities and ultimately to the wider community through publication of league tables – has brought the ethos of the free market into school management. If children's exam scores fail to measure up, parents vote with their feet; if Ofsted finds a school wanting, it has to shape up or face serious consequences.

Today, if you were to ask educationalists – policy makers, inspectors, headteachers and classroom teachers – for one word to describe the policy zeitgeist, it's likely they would reply *standards*. And chances are that if you were to ask students for one word to describe how their lives at school could be improved, they would come up with that most misused and loaded of words: respect. The two concepts are tightly interwoven.

Respect is a tricky concept, as subjective as they come. But, as the government has acknowledged in the Education Act 2002, a universally recognised method of ensuring that children feel they are respected in schools is listening to what they have to say and giving them responsibility that has genuine value. The idea of respect breeding respect may seem self-evident. But my own and others' research in the UK and the United States has shown time and again that children and young people who are on the margins of the education system or who have left it altogether speak of the lack of respect for students in their schools and the negative impact it has had on them. They recount stories, in humiliation as much as in anger, of teachers who are sarcastic, negative or indifferent but nonetheless demand respectfulness, a positive attitude and commitment (Klein, 1999).

With young people's hypocrisy barometers forever on full alert, schools can't have it both ways. Introducing student involvement into the equation means that staff are more accountable in their day to day dealings with students. And when those interactions become more transparent and positive, not only do students respond in kind but teachers find that they are more honest with themselves in their professional life and more positive about their jobs.

For a proportion of schools, giving students a voice in the way they experience education will be a major challenge. Many children and young people have been consigned to a passive role at school. The government determines what is to be learned, schools determine how the learning is to be delivered and governors determine by whom.

As the Euridem Project Review of Pupil Democracy in Europe put it in 2000:

> .... in England and in Wales, children neither have the right to be involved in matters such as school choice, curriculum and appeals over permanent exclusions nor in the broader issues of school or educational policy. There is no requirement to involve children in decisions on, for example, school uniform, arrangements for school meals, supervision in the playground, tackling bullying or discipline. There has been minimal consultation with pupils on the National Curriculum or teaching methods. The School Standards and Framework Act 1998 requires the governing bodies of schools to introduce behaviour policies but requires only headteachers and parents to be consulted. Schools are not required to introduce complaints procedures and only a minority have school councils within which to consult children and ensure that their views are reflected in the development of policy. There are examples of imaginative and democratic school councils, cross-school behaviour policies and peer counselling schemes in which pupils themselves take an active part in tackling and challenging bullying or racism in schools. Yet there is no consistent legal framework for their development and no statutory obligation to give children participation rights in schools. The QCA curriculum for citizenship, while demanding the 'knowledge, skills and values relevant to the nature and practice of participative democracy' falls short of advocating democratic structures, such as school councils as statutory. (Davies L and Kirkpatrick G, 2000)

The philosophical ground has shifted considerably since then with the introduction of the Education Act 2002. It is fair to say that it is the most far-reaching education legislation so far in terms of addressing the role of students in the education process. The Consortium on Education, a group of children's rights organisations led by Save the Children UK, lobbied Parliament for over a year to include a legal requirement within the Education Act to take into account the views of students on matters that affect them. It produced an amendment to the then Bill, which attracted much support from ministers and civil servants. In the end, the Act included the Consortium's amendment. Although it is not itself a statutory requirement, the government has put a duty on schools and local education authorities to have 'due regard' to the regulations of the Secretary of State on pupil participation. In other words, schools and LEAs are required to comply with the DfES guidance on pupil participation and will be inspected on their enactment of it.

The Labour government appears determined to break through some of the conventions that have kept children and young people shut out of democratic processes to date. In addition to the Education Act, the introduction of Education for Citizenship to secondary schools in September 2002 has brought on board a powerful engine driving active participation and democracy in schools.

These moves are being buttressed and enhanced by other government initiatives, too. The Children's and Young People's Unit in the Department for Education and Skills is committed, according to its consultation document, to listening to and acting on the views of young people through all government departments. Its principles for children and young people's policies and services include:

- taking into account the child's or young person's wishes and feelings

- children and young people having opportunities to play an effective role in the design and delivery of policies and services

The CYPU, in one of the most concerted and coherent attempts to make children's and young people's services joined up and accountable to its consumers, requires all government departments to adhere to core principles for the participation of youth in government. Each department has been asked to publish an action plan laying out how it intends to adopt these core principles to increase young people's participation. Yearly assessments and reports on the impact of those principles and the degree to which children and young people are encouraged to participate in policy-making and service delivery will be made by the Children and Young People's Unit.

This book aims to consolidate thinking on participation, generate ideas on how to achieve it and encourage their use. It refers to, among other things, the four countries included in the Euridem Project – Germany, Denmark, Sweden and the Netherlands – which is a study of students' rights enshrined in quite detailed legislation. In those countries, laws demand specific structures both in schools and outside them to enable children and young people to exercise their full rights and representation through a number of sophisticated channels.

Our legislation falls short of that. But with the DfES's forthcoming guidance on pupil participation promising to be groundbreaking in tone and broad in scope, the opportunities are there to push boundaries. This book offers examples of how schools have already being pushing boundaries and opening up to include students as active partners.

Practising what it preaches
The guidance is also groundbreaking in conception, being developed in consultation with two advisory groups. One group is made up of twelve young people from primary, secondary and special schools who workshop ideas on various aspects of school management (for instance budgets, school environment, curriculum, policies). Their

ideas are fed into the draft guidance together with those of the second advisory group, which is made up of statutory and non-statutory bodies including teachers' and head-teachers' organisations, Save the Children, Ofsted, the National Children's Bureau and the Citizenship Foundation.

But the guidance is not intended to supersede existing policy arrangements at individual schools. It will still be up to schools to decide their own policies, although they will have to take account of the guidance in doing so. The guidance exists to help schools decide when and how best to involve students in establishing policies. So though, for instance, students in primary and secondary schools facing exclusion still have no automatic rights to attend meetings of the discipline committee, the guidance will show schools how students can participate in developing policy that will give them greater rights in the exclusion process.

The law on children's rights
From a legislative point of view, there is plenty to support children's participation apart from the Education Act 2002. Perhaps most far-reaching is the groundbreaking UN Convention on the Rights of the Child introduced in 1989. The following points relate most directly to student participation:

Article 29
    ...the education of the child shall be directed to...the preparation of the child for responsible life in a free society, in the spirit of understanding, peace, tolerance, equality of sexes and friendship among all peoples, ethnic, national and religious groups and persons of indigenous origin.

Article 12
    Provides for a child's participation in decisions affecting him or her (assuming they are capable of forming their own views) and the right to express their views freely in all matters affecting them, including the right to be heard in any judicial or administrative proceedings affecting them.

Article 13

Gives children the right to obtain and make known information and to express their views, unless this violates the right of others.

Article 42

Gives a clear mandate to educators to develop methods which help children learn about their rights by appropriate and active means.

The Human Rights Act, which came into force in October 2000, also has a number of articles relating to children's role in schools, including:

Article 9

Freedom of thought, conscience and religion. This conflicts with education legislation, which prohibits children themselves opting out of religious education and worship in schools, giving that right to parents only.

Participation and the drive for inclusion

Despite the advances in standards in recent years, there remains a significant minority of children for whom school doesn't work. In England, just over a quarter of students left school without achieving A to C grades in their GCSE exams in the 2000–2001 school year; and nearly 20% of 16–25 year olds are neither in school nor in the workforce (Department for Education and Skills, 2001).

But even those who are getting on with their education find that schools leave some room for improvement. A number of studies on pupils' views of school conducted in this country over the last five years have found varying degrees of dissatisfaction with school. Some cited frustration at not having more of a choice in the subjects they studied (Joseph Rowntree Foundation, 2001). Another survey of over 2,000 students aged seven to 17 found that 40% of those questioned felt that they had too few rights at school. Many of them said they wanted opportunities to play a part in their school community (ESRC, 1999).

In an inspired and revealing small scale survey of primary and secondary school children's views that Save the Children undertook in response to the Government's Green Paper *Building on Success* in June 2001, the majority of secondary school children said that rules and codes of behaviour were developed by teachers without students being brought into the process. One young person's comment sums up the way many students see their place in the hierarchical school structure.

> Teachers have made the rules and don't really discuss with children. There are too many sets of rules. Teachers always think they are right and are not willing to compromise. (Save the Children, 2001)

Not just a philosophy

There is virtually no data to prove that student participation enhances attainment. But surveys and anecdotal evidence from headteachers and other senior managers strongly suggest that this is the case. Educationalists say that a participative school builds students' self-esteem, their motivation to learn and their connectedness with learning and the school, all of which enhance their school experience. In addition, in those schools where there are effective and active student councils and other programmes designed to offer students experiences of meaningful participation, there are lower rates of truancy than in similar schools which do not run such programmes. Moreover, participative schools have fewer behaviour problems and more positive relationships between students and teachers than other schools of a similar profile (Hannam, 2001).

In his pilot study of twelve schools identified as being particularly participative, Derry Hannam spoke to staff and students who were in no doubt that the democratisation of their schools was a positive step. The schools differed widely from each other in the extent of involvement enjoyed by the students. At one school, the PSHE programme was completely rewritten by teachers working in collaboration with students and students evaluate teaching and learning systematically. At a small number of others, students participated in governors' meetings and student reps had voting rights on a sub-committee, as well as being involved in the appointment of staff and curriculum review procedures.

Hannam summarised the views of teachers on the impact student involvement had on their schools:

> The teachers believed that the participative activities were of great benefit to all students, whatever their gender, academic ability or social background and that working with these students, although often adding to their workload, was a major source of their job satisfaction. They commented upon improved attendance, enhanced self-esteem, motivation to learn and engagement with learning and attainment, although their evidence was largely anecdotal.

The students he surveyed were similarly positive and from their response he concludes that:

> Participative activities require students to take initiatives and decisions. This generates motivation, ownership and a sense of being independent, trusted and responsible. This supports the learning of communication and collaboration skills. These facilitate 'quality' outcomes which both intrinsically and through recognition from others lead to enhanced self-esteem. Out of this comes an overall sense of personal and social 'efficacy' – which is probably the *sine qua non* for the development of political efficacy, a major aim of the Citizenship Education Project.

> Students believe that involvement in participatory activities enhanced learning across the curriculum – sometimes in unexpected and unpredictable ways. In many cases students described the development of important organisational and time-

management skills in order to ensure that the participatory activities had no adverse effect on their 'regular' schoolwork. (Hannam, 2001)

Of all the participative structures and activities in schools' repertoires, it is arguably an effective, representative student council that makes the greatest impact on the attitudes of students, particularly in their sense of connectedness with the school and the world outside it.

One single structure that appears to be most influential in a variety of dimensions of citizenship preparedness is the existence of and participation in a students' council. The simple existence of students' council at the school level seems associated with higher participation in other school activities ... and seems to encourage positive attitudes towards political pluralism. For those directly involved in managing the students' councils, the impact appears to be even more important; they attain higher levels of positive attitudes towards civic tolerance and political pluralism and tend to be more involved in out of school activities. (Abela-Bertrand, 1997)

Hannam's study also looked at measurable indicators of student participation. Taking data from the twelve schools and setting it against that of schools in similar circumstances that were not participative, he came to the following conclusions:

- the participative schools had significantly lower exclusion rates than the other schools

- attendance was slightly higher in the participative schools – although from some of the participative schools there was strong anecdotal evidence that attendance was significantly improved among boys

- collectively, GCSE results were higher than expected in the participative schools. This finding is corroborated by Ofsted, who looked at the results of the original sixteen schools in the study. Moreover, the gap between the participative schools and other schools is increasing year on year. For example, the proportion of schools expected to be judged as average or better than average (grades A*-C) is 60%. Collectively, the figure for the twelve schools in the sample was 67% for 1998 and 1999 and 92% for 2000. In 2000, half the participative schools achieved A-A*, whereas the expected figure is 25%.

But if the sketchy data that exists shows positive effects of student participation on behaviour and performance, the most compelling argument has to be the anecdotal feedback from students themselves. The substance of it is that they respond with maturity and responsibility to being listened to, seeing their suggestions and recommendations being acted upon and having a part in the running of their schools.

Save the Children's consultation paper on the Green Paper *Schools: Building on Success* surveyed primary and secondary school students for their views over a range of subjects, including whether they felt schools should have a charter of behaviour, school councils and a forum for students to have a say in how schools are run. There was strong support for schools having these mechanisms in place. Here's what some of them said:

> *Some pupils get the chance [to air their views] but not always.*

> *Teachers have made the rules and don't really discuss with children. There are too many sets of rules. I think schools should have a pupil council because they need to hear what we think and feel.*

> *It doesn't make a difference. We have a pupil council and they don't do nothing and are not acknowledged. Teachers always think they are right and are not willing to compromise.* (Save the Children, 2001)

But those schools that have managed to break through the barrier of tokenism into meaningful participation have done so with tremendous energy, enthusiasm, rigour and creativity. At Primrose Hill Primary School in Camden, north London, for instance, children aged four to eleven sit on a highly effective school council. In the last few years, it has tackled the following issues, often fundraising to raise cash for the changes they wish to see:

- *Unsatisfactory school lunches.* The school council wrote to the catering manager about the quality and quantity of the food and improvements were made as a result.

- *The school playground.* Children aired their dissatisfaction with the uninviting bare space and it has consequently been redeveloped in line with the children's recommendations, including outdoor murals painted on the perimeter walls by the children.

- *The quality of school toilets.* The school council campaigned and won new toilets for the school.

The school council is just one of a multi-pronged programme of activities at Primrose Hill School designed to give more rights and responsibilities to the children. Citizenship is embedded in the ethos of the school and is a high profile focal point for training of both teachers and children. The schoolchildren have worked with CSV (Community Service Volunteers) on collaborative projects in which they have been given role-play exercises to train them in listening and negotiation techniques. They have also learned how to publicise their fundraising activities, write press releases and liaise with newspapers.

Circle time is another bedrock of the participative ethos of the school. It is there where the building blocks are laid down for learning how to respect each other, to listen to each other and to accept differences.

As one ten year old girl put it:

At our school, we're kind to each other. Even if someone says something silly or if we don't agree with it, it's their right to say it without people laughing at them or saying rude things.

At Colne Community School in Brightlingsea, Essex, students are given their rights and responsibilities within the school in the conventional ways, including a thriving school council and circle time until Year 9. They have also been involved in less usual activities, including the following:

- A peer education project in which volunteers are trained by youth workers on a week-long residential course to go out to the local junior school to run sessions raising awareness of drug and alcohol misuse. There is a similar scheme in which sixth formers teach Year 9s.

- Change Makers, run in PSHE for all Year 7s, in which students devise a project themselves that will make a difference to the school or local community.

- Service learning/active learning. Students do a needs assessment of their community to determine where there are improvements needed and then develop a project, linked to the curriculum in some way, that will address it.

By connecting with the community, students learn about rights and responsibilities in the wider sense – and about their potential power as members of civil society to change things than require changing. A Year 8 student told me about a project he and others had been involved with.

We went on a school council programme with other schools and decided to work on improving public spaces where young people hang out. We decided to develop a skate park. We got shown different designs for shelters and chose one that we liked but we only had £1,000 to spend so we're still working on it. Maybe we'll have to compromise and put in fewer than we had originally planned.

Another Year 8 student described a coup that the local Youth Forum, of which Colne School is a member, pulled off:

We spoke to the bus manager about the prices that young people have to pay being too high. We managed to get them to reduce the fares for 14 to 16 year olds and now young people get their bus passes for free.

How the curriculum supports participation
Education for Citizenship, which became compulsory in secondary schools in September 2002, makes a cogent and immediate argument for student participation and offers the means to achieve it to some extent.

Equipping children with the critical and cognitive tools to communicate their points of view and make decisions for themselves signifies a seismic philosophical shift in education in this country. ...'good education' is now being interpreted through the new national curriculum orders for citizenship education as empowering children to not only understand the concept of rights but to learn what their rights are and what their role is in ensuring those rights are met in order to fulfil their own educational potential. The message inherent in the curriculum framework is that citizenship is not just about preparing children to become active citizens when they are older; it's about acknowledging that they are part of society today, that they are aware of the world in which they live and that they are eager to take their place in it. (Klein, 2001)

The Education for Citizenship orders contain three strands, two of which relate directly to participation. By assuming social and moral responsibility both in and beyond the classroom, children are being asked to engage with their learning environment: to improve it, to speak out against what they disagree with, to cast an analytical eye over what goes on around them. Being involved in the community is arguably as much to do with the community of the school as with what goes on outside its gates. Both strands encourage a sense of active engagement with the institutions and structures that circumscribe children's lives.

If citizenship education is to have any meaning, it has to place learning about rights and responsibilities, political frameworks and democratic society squarely within the realm of experience. It is as much about doing as learning about. And if participation is to have any meaning, it has to be set in *frameworks* that have real meaning. An obvious vehicle for this is school councils, structures in which children have the opportunity to exercise their rights and experience the democratic process at first hand. Their existence in a school is the key indicator of democracy in a school. A 1999 research study carried out by the ESRC into children's knowledge of civil rights in schools found that half the 2,272 pupils questioned had a school council at their school but only 20 per cent thought theirs was effective and 28% felt that it was ineffective. (ESRC, 1999)

Unless the councils have an actual role, are truly representative of the student body and are taken seriously by other students as well as staff and parents, they are dismissed by everybody and, worse, they engender cynicism and alienation. As one child interviewed by Save the Children for its children's eye-view response to the then Green Paper remarked:

> *We have a pupil council and it doesn't make a difference. They don't do nothing and are not acknowledged. Teachers always think they are right and are not willing to compromise.*

Another child, when interviewed for a research project on school councils and exclusions, voiced the feeling of being on the outside that can arise from unrepresentative school councils:

> *The wrong ones are picked for the council. They listen to their own friends. It's always their way. No one listens.* (School Councils UK, 1999)

Student participation and the school improvement agenda

The connection between giving children a voice in schools and enhanced school effectiveness is woefully under-researched. But what research does exist points to a strong correlation.

The Euridem Project is arguably the most solid research study in this area. A review of pupil democracy in Denmark, Sweden, the Netherlands and Germany, it looks not only at the legislative frameworks that underpin school democracy but also at how the different models that are used in these diverse systems impact on the educational and social aspects of the school.

What emerges from this genuinely uplifting report is a picture of shared respect and humanity between teachers and students that engenders harmony, good behaviour and engagement with learning. While none of the four systems was found to be perfect, what the researchers found was that:

> When pupils had a voice and were accorded value, the school was a happier place; when pupils are happy and given dignity, they attend more and they work more productively...

> Outcomes are affected at a number of levels: individual children's experience and self-esteem as a learner; an enhanced change for the whole school; and the impact on wider society and social structures. (Davies and Kirkpatrick, 2000)

When pupils grow up with an open, listening and mutually respectful culture in schools from primary level on up as they do in Germany, the Netherlands, Denmark and Sweden, their confidence and self-esteem is strong and an ultimate consequence of this is that they behave better. It means that they attend school regularly. And when the law requires them to take part in curriculum planning and to evaluate and assess teaching standards, as the law in these countries does, they are more connected with their learning, seeing the relevance of the curriculum and taking more responsibility for their learning. They are more socially adept, too, because of their cooperative and collaborative work with fellow students on curriculum negotiation groups and other committees.

These countries have a thing or two to learn from British schools, too – primarily in terms of the decentralisation of schools under local management and also managing and celebrating cultural diversity and providing, as the UK does, a relatively advanced level of ICT in schools. And what lessons can we take from the Euridem Project? Well, for one thing, the report states that if true student democracy is ever to be realised here, it needs to be embedded in law rather than subject to interpretation. Student democracy is not going to happen to the extent that it has in the European countries documented in the project under current legislation in the UK. But in the absence of it, there is enormous scope for new thinking and new ways of working. Schools are being encouraged to think in broader sweeps about how students can become active partners in the planning, curriculum and delivery of education.

But encouraging these shifts by law is one thing. Changing the culture in schools is another.

CHAPTER 2
International perspectives

The Euridem Project is arguably the most solid research study investigating the connection between pupil participation and school effectiveness (see page 6 and 17). What emerges from the report is a picture of shared respect between teachers and students that fosters harmony, good behaviour and engagement with learning. While none of the four systems was found to be perfect, what the researchers found was that:

> When pupils had a voice and were accorded value, the school was a happier place; when pupils are happy and given dignity, they attend more and they work more productively...

> Outcomes are affected at a number of levels: individual children's experience and self-esteem as a learner; an enhanced change for the whole school; and the impact on wider society and social structures. (Davies and Kirkpatrick, 2000)

When pupils grow up with an open, listening and mutually respectful culture in their schools from primary level on up as they do in the four countries in the report, their confidence and self-esteem is stronger, their behaviour is better and their attendance is more regular. And when the law requires them to take part in curriculum planning and to evaluate and assess teaching standards, as it does in these countries, students are more connected with their learning.

They see the relevance of the curriculum and take more responsibility for their education. They are more socially adept, too, through working cooperatively and collaboratively with their peers on curriculum negotiation groups and other committees.

Findings of the Euridem Report

The Project was commissioned by the Children's Rights Alliance for England, carried out by the University of Birmingham's Centre for International Education and Research and published as a report in 2000. The purpose of the project was to collect data on:

- the law
- top-down views (from government officials to student union representatives) on student involvement and the effectiveness of the legislation
- observations of classes, school councils or participatory committees and interviews with pupils, teachers, heads and parents

In general terms, the researchers found that in these four countries student involvement in the decision-making process in their schools is enshrined in quite detailed law. Not only are schools legally bound to have student councils (which in many schools have their own allocated room with telephone and computer), but pupils must be represented on their governing bodies and other committees in the school and on local, regional and national levels. Students must also be involved in planning the curriculum and teaching in their own personal learning plans and those of the school. There are clearly laid out channels for all pupils to have their say.

In each country, school student unions are well organised and vocal. As well as running on government funding, they have the ear of the government at times of new education legislation and are also respected lobbyists for improvements to the education system.

The school ethos in the four countries is generally congenial and warm, characterised by open and mutually respectful relationships between teachers and students. Students were, moreover, confident and articulate about human rights, their rights as children and how to exercise them.

The following offers snapshot profiles of how students' rights are upheld in each of the four countries in the project.

Denmark

Denmark arguably has the most radical democratic structures in its schools of anywhere in Europe. Teaching and learning takes place within a dialogue culture, in which discussions are a major part of class time. All schools, basic (ages 6-16) and upper secondary (post 16), are informal places where students and teachers have easy but respectful relations with each other. As part of the 'anti-labelling' ideology first introduced in the 1930s, marks are viewed with suspicion by teachers; a student's ability to cooperate in the group work that forms a large part of each day can be seen as a better benchmark for assessment than graded work.

The law demands that a school board (governing body) be established at every school. Two student representatives are elected to sit on the board alongside parents and teachers. Although they have full voting rights, they are not allowed to take part in matters concerning individual pupils or teachers. As part of the school board they are involved in deliberating on:

- how teaching is organised, what optional subjects are offered, how many lessons are required
- school/home links
- how work is distributed between teaching staff

- the school budget
- teaching materials and school rules
- recommendations on staff appointments

The law also requires schools above a certain size and all upper secondary schools to establish a students' council appointed by pupils which, among other things, reports to the headteacher on general issues related to pupils.

Internal, class by class assessments of teaching are regularly carried out by teachers and students – also by law – along with regular discussion of teaching. These also evaluate the student-teacher interactions that take place in the the classroom. The substance of these assessments is not seen or used beyond the classroom.

Members of student councils in upper secondary schools are offered a seat on virtually any committee they wish to join, giving them potential powers unheard of in most other countries.

While the democratic freedoms are most marked in the upper schools, some basic (6-16) schools have decided for themselves that children want and deserve more of a voice and have created systems to make sure they get it. One such school asked each class to develop its own discipline policy. In addition, the children decide what work to do during free periods and are consulted by the teacher on future projects.

One Danish teacher in the Euridem study spoke of how the sharing of responsibilities and powers impacts on the school:

> *Living and behaving in a democratic way ... is a way of teachers talking ... not about voting in elections ... about kids having the right to talk and to be listened to ... that's a good teacher, a good classroom and probably a good school.*

When the Danish Ministry of Education sent a questionnaire to chairs of student councils in upper secondary schools, the response was generally optimistic although all said they wanted more representative student participation and more commitment from their peers. Many also spoke of the need for students to have greater influence on their schools. There is a general feeling that while there are active students within each school community who are representing the student body and helping to make their collective voice heard, it is within the context of a largely indifferent or sceptical majority – much the same as out in the real world.

Germany
In the Nord-Rhein Westfalen region included in the Euridem Project report there is no student representation on committees (student councils) at primary level, but there are varying degrees at secondary, depending on the type of school. Students also sit on curriculum subject committees with parents and teachers, to deal with frameworks and evaluation, suggestions on resources and on how subject rooms and workstations are arranged. There are also class and year councils, each with student representation alongside parents and teachers. These bodies participate in overseeing teaching, setting the type and extent of homework, assessment and other matters. Finally, there is also a student council.

Numerous opportunities exist for students to have their voices heard through these various channels. But sometimes the good old-fashioned method of protest and demonstration makes the strongest impact. The Euridem report includes an anecdote of a comprehensive school in the state of Nord-Rhein Westfalen that was to get a new prefab from the state government. Students opposed this move on environmental grounds and after demonstrating, were pleased to win the case: the school now has an ecologically designed building.

A degree of student autonomy is a hallmark of the system, whereby everyone has two free hours a week for project work, with the option of group work. Together with the teacher, they decide on the aims, methods and outcome of the project. They may choose to carry out this work in a self-learning centre at the school, where they can go during free time or during lessons.

Students are all part of different teams comprised of teachers, counsellors or parents, that take responsibility for a particular facility in the school – for instance the library, sports hall or ICT room. The aim is to get students to be participants in the school community and for them to acquire the confidence and training to lead single lessons. Weekend seminars for students, pupils and teachers are run to train them and help them acquire a variety of skills that will help them influence their school.

In Germany, students don't have the power to decide the curriculum or appoint staff as they have in Denmark. That being so, schools themselves decide how to create meaningful democratic opportunities and structures for their pupils.

As one headteacher told the researchers, it's a challenge that has its moments, but it's one worth taking:

> *It is sometimes not very comfortable for us. There are many ways in which pupils and students can oppose what we want. We have to discuss. But that is democracy.* (Headteacher, S. Comprehensive, Nord-Rhein Westfalen)

Sweden

There is an emphasis in legislation on democratic working structures as the *modus operandi* of everyone working in Swedish schools. The goal of all schools is to ensure that students:

- take responsibility for their work and their working environment

- take a progressively active role in influencing their learning and also the internal workings of the school

- understand democratic principles and how to be active citizens

School staff are required by law to facilitate children's influence on the way the school is run and what is taught; and there is an understanding that this influence should grow as the child grows older. Teachers also work with pupils on planning and evaluating their teaching.

Students sit on local boards, which offers them genuine opportunities to exert their influence on matters such as teacher appointments, planning in-service training and budget allocations. Curriculum planning is shared by student representatives and school staff.

There are also student councils at both lower and upper levels of the schools (children generally attend the same school from ages 6-16). The nature of the councils varies from school to school. Among the younger age groups, they deal mainly with minor issues. But one school quoted in the research had a budget for the lower school's student council. Higher up the school, weighty decisions such as the hiring and firing of staff and whole school budgets were in the hands of the older students.

But still, with all the legislative weight and positive ethos going for them, some Swedish students, like the Germans, Danish, Dutch, and like the British, Americans and Japanese as well, hang back, preferring to let others be active, take decisions, get involved. To counter this trend, one Swedish school quoted in the report set up a student participation committee of teachers and pupils to address the issue of how to get all students to participate and exercise their rights. This led to a sophisticated structure called 'workteams,' which was a way of scaling down the large school, personalising relationships between teachers and students and thereby motivating students to get involved in negotiations with teachers on teaching methods, homework, tests, etc. Taking responsibility for their own learning through this level of involvement is perceived as being more important for the development of less active students than sitting on committees and setting budgets.

The Netherlands

The Dutch government maintains a centralised education policy over decentralised schools. One of the principle roles of education, as enshrined in national policy, is preparing young people for democratic citizenship and responsibilities and building their personalities.

Students are given a great deal of autonomy. From the age of 15, they have the opportunity to choose the subjects they want to study. They choose whether to work in groups or on their own on projects and they plan their educational activities. This way of working configures with the concept of the virtual school recently presented by the UK's Department for Education and Skills, where teachers evolve into facilitators and supporters rather than serving as the purveyors of a curriculum.

All schools must by law set up a participation council; only in the secondary schools does this include student representation but at both primary and secondary it involves parents. These bodies have certain powers, including approval rights over school board decisions in certain matters.

In addition to the participation councils, secondary school pupils have powers to set up a student council which can work closely with the separate parents' council.

Schools are also legally mandated to write a code of conduct setting out the rights and responsibilities of pupils, known as the Pupil's Charter. This document has to be revised by the school board every two years and is subject to the approval of pupils and parents on the participation council.

A national action committee promotes student participation in schools by helping schools set up student councils. Its guide to secondary schools for parents and pupils offers a checklist on questions to ask a prospective school about democratic practice.

Conclusion

The composite picture that emerges from the Euridem Project is one of state governments putting a great deal of thought into legislation and money into such things as student council unions, to ensure that that their school-aged citizens learn about their democratic rights by having a variety of opportunities in which to exercise them. But just as importantly, there is an ethos within the education community of these countries that supports the concept of democratic schools. There is also an acceptance that although this may not be the easiest way of running schools, it is not only the fairest but also the most likely to get the best from the students.

CHAPTER 3

The building blocks, the stumbling blocks

It is obvious that all formal preparation for citizenship in adult life can be helped or hindered by the ethos and organisation of a school, whether pupils are given opportunities for exercising responsibilities and initiatives or not; and whether they are consulted realistically on matters where their opinions can prove relevant both to the efficient running of a school and to their general motivation for learning. In some schools these are already common practices, while in others, they are absent or only occasional. (QCA, 1998)

Some European states, as we have seen, have established and embedded sophisticated legislation enshrining student rights and mandating schools to be more democratic. Britain has come more recently to the promotion of greater involvement of young people in their education, largely in response to the groundswell of pressure from a coalition of non-statutory children's rights and education reform bodies, among others. However, non-statutory guidance leaves the implementation of such policies up to individual schools.

There have been other efforts over the years to change the climate in education. Among them was a policy statement in 1972 from the short-lived National Union of School

Students, formed under the auspices of the National Union of Students, that signified 'what must rank as one of the most uncompromising and idealistic statements of liberation philosophy ever seen in British educational politics' (Wagg, 1996). It called for systemic changes to the way schools are run, including 'an increase of student responsibility and self-discipline in schools,' for school rules to be published and for a school committee to have jurisdiction over disciplinary procedures.

Perhaps the single most important incursion into the complex area – some might say minefield – of giving children and young people some control over their lives and the structures in which they live them came with Britain's signing of the UN Convention on the Rights of the Child in 1991. This signalled a major departure from the zeitgeist that had until relatively recently been content to continue to consign school pupils to the role, in the words of an Anthony Powell character, 'of uneasy, stranded beings' (quoted in Rudduck and Flutter, 2000). With ratification of the Convention came an acceptance that children and young people had not only responsibilities but rights, too, that they were capable of handling with seriousness and maturity.

If the government has stopped short of mandating more rights for students in straightforward legislation, it does seem to be attuned to the concept of children's participation in this as in other areas of their lives. In its document *Learning to Listen, Core Principles for the Involvement of Children and Young People* (2001), the Children and Young People's Unit emphasises the government's commitment to putting in place policies and services across all departments that are shaped by the needs and views of children and young people. In another document, the consultation paper entitled *Building a Strategy for Children and Young People*, the Unit states:

> We want all of our children and young people to be assured of chances to contribute to their local communities – feeling heard and being valued as responsible citizens – shaping their lives and their futures.

Wales and Scotland have the lead on England in this respect. In its consultation document on services for children and young people, the Welsh Assembly proposes that:

1. all service provision for children and young people be informed by the United Nations Convention on the Rights of the Child

2. children and young people should be listened to and their views acted upon

3. all primary and secondary schools in Wales should set up school councils

The Standards in Scotland's Schools Act 2000 places a duty on local education authorities to listen to the views of children and young people in decisions that significantly affect them (taking into account their age and maturity) and gives pupils the opportunity to make their views known vis a vis their school's annual development plans.

We look at the structural and cultural barriers to achieving children and young people's participation towards the end of this chapter. But first, let's look at the the channels through which primary and secondary students are already taking their place as partners in their education.

Education for Citizenship: vehicle for school democracy or damp squib?

The aim of education for citizenship, which was introduced as a new national curriculum subject at key stages 3 and 4 in August 2002, is to give pupils the knowledge, skills and understanding they need to become informed, active and responsible members of their community, whether that community is the micro world of the school, their locality, the country or far beyond national borders. In the words of the Speaker's Commission on Citizenship, created by former speaker of the House Bernard Wetherill, to adopt the role of citizens in adulthood, students

> ...need to have the skills to question and evaluate; to argue, debate and protest; to resolve conflict without resorting to violence and to work collaboratively. They need to understand society and how it works, especially their rights and responsibilities within it. They need to recognise themselves as being part of a community and respect others within that community. (Weatherill, 1990)

An international study of citizenship education in 29 countries at age 14 (Kerr *et al*, 2002) shows just what a complex combination of skills is required and how sophisticated and multi-layered the pedagogy needs to be to teach the subject in a meaningful way. The study reveals that while England has, until now, lagged behind the other countries by not having civic or citizenship education in its statutory school curriculum, the way it is delivered in most of those other countries shows we haven't missed out on much. While the facts may be taught to students around the world, the approach to citizenship is conventional, characterised by talk and chalk as opposed to being open and participatory; only a quarter of students surveyed across the 29 countries said they were often encouraged to air their opinions during classroom discussion in citizenship lessons; an equal proportion said this happened rarely if ever. This highlights the fact that citizenship education is very much in the hands of the practitioner. Of all the subjects in the curriculum, it has the potential to be the most influential on students' attitudes and behaviour as well as being experiential in that it offers teachers and students the chance to engage with the outside world. It provides routes through which students can put theory into practice and, in the process, impact on their learning and physical environment. The notion of rights and responsibilities becomes realised when opportunities are created to make decisions and see them through. Because of this, it has the power to engage the disengaged with their school, community and more generally with the notion of active citizenship.

But if citizenship has the potential to do all these things, it also has the makings of being a colossal missed opportunity. If headteachers and staff fail to approach it positively and do not plough into its planning the rigour and energy required to maximise its possibilities, education for citizenship will be nothing more than a glorified civics module. For citizenship to be learned, it has to be experienced. And experience is about participation in discussion, in the formulation of ideas and plans, in realising that their contribution counts and has an impact.

The Education for Citizenship orders contain three strands, two of which relate directly to participation. By assuming social and moral responsibility both in and beyond the class-room, children are being asked to engage with their learning environment; to improve it, to speak out against what they disagree with, to cast an analytical eye over what goes on around them. Being involved in the community is arguably as much to do with the community of the school as with what goes on outside its gates. Both strands encourage a sense of active engagement with the institutions and structures that circumscribe children's lives:

> Equipping children with the critical and cognitive tools to communicate their points of view and make decisions for themselves signifies a seismic philosophical shift in education in this country. ... 'good education' is now being interpreted through the new national curriculum orders for citizenship education as empowering children to not only understand the concept of rights but to learn what their rights are and what their role is in ensuring those rights are met in order to fulfil their own educational potential. The message inherent in the curriculum framework is

that citizenship is not just about preparing children to become active citizens when they are older; it's about acknowledging that they are part of society today, that they are aware of the world in which they live and that they are eager to take their place in it. (Klein, 2001)

When children and young people feel that their views are being sought and listened to and when they are given the freedom, within reason, to redress or improve the unsatisfactory or to create things where nothing existed before, a world of possibilities opens to them. Most importantly, they see that they have the power to change things. At a time when the apathy of young voters on both sides of the Atlantic is vexing society as a whole, that is an important lesson.

While citizenship education is the natural platform from which to encourage participatory attitudes, schools themselves have divergent views on what these lessons should be prioritising and what they should not. In a survey sent out to 10,000 primary, middle and secondary schools in England, Scotland, Wales and Northern Ireland and, significantly, replied to by only 400, schools were asked to rank different elements of the content and practice of citizenship education into order of priority.

The picture that emerged was that, in terms of content, schools gave a lower priority to democratic models, topical issues and values and were more positive about global issues and human rights. In terms of practice, they rated understanding rights as by far and away the most important components of the curriculum; the lowest were community service and community participation.

As Unicef itself admits in the report of the survey (Unicef, 2000), it is difficult to know precisely how to interpret these findings, since the terms are ambiguous and the distinction between content and practice can be blurred. Why, for instance, do 83% of the schools give high priority to helping pupils to understand their rights and responsibilities in practice while only 48% prioritise human rights concepts and instruments as part of curriculum content?

But given these complexities, it is a useful window through which to look at the way schools were thinking about citizenship education prior to its formal introduction in autumn 2002. It should also be a wake-up call to citizenship educators and publishers of teaching materials about the weak areas in schools' approaches to the subject.

Most interestingly, the little work that has been done on children's and young people's views on what they want to learn in citizenship looks curiously at odds with schools' views of what is important and what isn't. A consultation carried out by Save the Children and the DfES with primary and secondary school students on the main themes of the then White Paper on Education (Save the Children, 2001) showed that:

1. students want to discuss topical issues and current affairs. *These were low priorities among schools in the Unicef study.*

2. students want to learn about politics. *This was a low priority in the Unicef study.*

3. students want to be involved in voluntary service. *This was a low priority in the Unicef study.*

Another study asked seven to 17 year olds what they knew about their civil rights and asked them and teachers how these rights related to schools. Its findings reveal that three quarters of the 2,272 students in the survey said they had not heard about the UN Convention on the Rights of the Child; the remainder said they had only heard 'a bit about it'. Children were aware of teachers avoiding having practical sessions on children's civil rights, opting instead for 'boring' and abstract discussions about democracy, justice and peace. As one eight year old memorably put it:

It's so boring when they keep telling you that making the world a better place means picking up litter and not killing whales.

Forty per cent of the children and 11 per cent of the teachers said that students don't have enough rights at school; many of the children said that 'they want to contribute more to their school community and be recognised as responsible, competent people.'

For this cohort, even being asked their views for the survey was liberating, giving them a rare experience of participation. Said one:

> We are never actually asked anything, we are just told we have got to do this and we have got to do that. It was nice [with the survey] to actually think that somebody was taking into consideration what you thought or wanted to say. (Alderson, 1999)

School Councils

If Citizenship Education is to have any meaning, it has to be placed firmly within the realm of students' experiences of democratic schools. Fielding (2001, p. 104) cautions:

> Unless teachers and pupils see the skills and capacities associated with the growth of student voice as integrally connected with the practical realities of democracy and democratic citizenship in the lived, day-to-day context of real schools as they exist now, then those skills will turn out to be virtually worthless. They will quickly become ephemeral tricks that not only have no genuine significance for those who use them, but, just as importantly, for those on whose behalf they have been developed.

An obvious vehicle for the practice of democratic citizenship is the school councils, a structure in which children have the opportunity to exercise their rights and experience first hand the democratic process.

While Britain remains the odd country out in the rest of Europe in not having legislation requiring schools to provide student councils, there are frameworks other than the DfES guidance on participation that make pointed reference to the important role these councils have to play in children's development. The Qualifications and Curriculum Authority (QCA), for one, recommends in its guidance that schools set up councils as part of their education for citizenship provision. And the education for citizenship orders, as we have seen, stress the need for schools to not only provide information about democratic processes but to offer opportunities to exercise them in meaningful ways, i.e. through school councils. The National Foundation for Educational Research has just completed a major piece of research on the role of school councils in citizenship and personal and social education (Taylor and Johnson, 2002).

Effective school councils can bring far-reaching benefits to pupils, teachers and the wider community. There are the more obvious advantages, such as providing participants with active learning experiences of democracy. But a school council has less apparent positive effects, too, such as moving the responsibility for enforcing good behaviour away from teachers and towards the school community as a whole. In the process, it has the potential to involve disaffected students, promoting a sense of ownership of the school (School Councils UK).

The existence of pupil or student councils is the prime indicator of children's participation in their school and a barometer of the priority that a school gives to children's rights. A school with a council is, for instance, a third more likely to consult students about school uniforms and equal opportunities issues (School Councils UK).

There are other vehicles schools can use for raising standards and encouraging children to participate in matters of school policy, such as circle time, peer mediation and class meetings. These are all good methods for helping children and young people develop the skills to find a voice, to understand that their opinion matters and to participate in meaningful and constructive ways. Taylor and Johnson (2002, p. 126) argue that:

> school councils must be embedded in school-wide relationships, structures and actions which are disposed towards consultation, respect for the views of students and staff, participation in the schools as a community, respect for reason, democracy and the possibility of change. It is not enough for the school council itself to be the only marker of such attitudes and behaviours. The school council needs to be one of many, albeit one of the most potentially fair and equal, opportunities for the exercise of students' rights and responsibilities within the experience of social and academic learning.

While school councils can provide an opportunity to develop a real understanding of citizenship, social inclusion in councils is a particularly important and problematic issue. Participation is tied up with many different factors, including self-esteem and self-image, and some schools face challenges in galvanising interest and involvement from groups of students who, for whatever reason, perceive themselves to be marginalised.

It is not known exactly how many school councils exist throughout the UK because there has never been an attempt to quantify them. But it is possible to extrapolate from a 1998 survey conducted by the National Society for the Prevention of Cruelty to Children that over a third of secondary schools in England and probably Wales have student councils. More recent estimates suggest that half of secondary schools now have them (Hannam in conversation, 2001a). The proportion of primary schools running councils is far fewer. It is likely that the overall numbers will rise as a result of citizenship education because of its emphasis on the experiential dimension of learning about democracy and on acquiring skills enabling them to participate and take responsible action.

When schools are participative, they seem, in the words of Derry Hannam,

> to square the circle of authority and compulsion with real freedom and responsibility. They appear to be able to create an ethos where education for democracy is experientially possible and by so doing, enhance the ethos in such a way that makes it progressively more possible. My impression as an [Ofsted] inspector has been that although significant staff time is indeed devoted to supporting the activities that create the democratic ethos of these schools, there appears to be no price tag being paid in conventionally measured attainment. On the contrary, it appears that some students who might otherwise give up on school learning develop a renewed sense of purpose in an environment that raises their self-esteem through the sharing of trust, responsibility and participation in decision-making. (Hannam, 2001b)

And when councils are good, they are valued by students as a vehicle for improving conditions, ie, the school environment and on school policy, such as rules and codes of behaviour. In Hannam's study, headteachers and other senior managers expressed their belief that participation

> ...impacts beneficially on self-esteem, motivation, sense of ownership and empowerment and that this in turn enhances attainment [among] students whatever their gender, academic ability or social background and that working with these students, although often adding to their workload, was a major source of job satisfaction.(Hanman, 2001b)

Headteachers and staff in another study looking at school councils and pupil exclusions (Davies, 1999) were impressed and sometimes surprised at the performance of student councillors, including those in primary schools. They spoke of their articulacy and ability to grasp and operate within the principles and boundaries of the democratic process. In addition, they believed that having a school council had a positive effect on pupils' behaviour, on teachers' willingness to listen to pupils' views and, following on from those things, on school ethos generally.

But there are councils and councils. Nearly 30 per cent of the students questioned in the Civil Rights in Schools Project (Alderson, 1999) said that theirs was ineffectual or tokenistic. Another study of primary and secondary schools found that the majority of students had mixed views on their school council. While some felt that it made a genuine contribution to formulating policy, others did not believe that it had the power to effect genuine change (Davies, 1999).

Eight year old primary schoolchildren, it seems, are able to distinguish between truly democratic councils and those that were not. They are also able to listen to one another, to take minutes, brainstorm, provide creative solutions to problems and resolve disagreements through peaceful inter-ventions. It has been demonstrated, too, that even infant school children are capable of demonstrating sophisticated skills when adults encourage them, have high expectations of them and work together with them on school councils (Alderson, 2000).

As one child interviewed by Save the Children for its chil-dren's eye view response to the then Green Paper remarked:

> *We have a pupil council and it doesn't make a difference. They don't do nothing and are not acknowledged. Teachers always think they are right and are not willing to compromise.*

Surveys of students undertaken by Save the Children England (2001) reveal dissatisfaction with:

- school councils having little real influence over im-portant matters and not being representative of the student body

- teachers not listening to or consulting with students on rules and codes of behaviour

- the lack of freedom that students have to choose the subjects they want to study

- their lack of representation on disciplinary boards

- not having the voice to influence the way the curriculum is delivered; for instance, in the provision of more practical work in subjects

Interestingly, the existence of a school council that does nothing not only fools nobody but can actually backfire. When a school council is perceived by pupils as being tokenistic and purely cosmetic, it can do more harm than good.

> Simply starting a council, without ensuring that other aspects of the school improve, does not necessarily improve a school. It could increase disaffection about the tensions between rhetoric and democracy and reality in school life and about the school generally. Setting up a democratic council with the students involves related changes throughout the school in routines and relationships.(NFER, 2002)

A recent survey of primary and secondary school children conducted by Save the Children (Save the Children, 2001) reveals that students whose schools ran school councils largely found them ineffective and 'decorative.' In their eyes, apathy on the part of the student body as well as ineffective management of the councils were to blame.

But despite this, students are generally upbeat about the potential for councils to act as a forum for their voices to be heard about issues concerned with school life, from the choice of equipment being bought to school trips, to discipline and hiring staff. In other words, their disillusionment with the reality of councils has not diminished their enthusiasm for them in principle. They believe that, given the right circumstances, student councils can work to their benefit.

SEN Code of Practice

The expanded guidance to the Code of Practice puts a premium on students having a say in their own learning and school experience. For the first time, children and young people with special needs are being actively encouraged by education policy to be involved in planning what services they receive at school and in communicating their views on how they should be delivered.

The guidance and accompanying SEN Toolkit are models for pupil participation in all aspects of education. So much so, in fact, that the DfES has said that it will use it as a model for the guidance on participation. In its introduction to Section 3 of the Code of Practice on pupil participation, it sets its philosophical position by quoting the UN Convention on the Rights of the Child:

> Children, who are capable of forming views, have a right to receive and make known information, to express an opinion and to have that opinion taken into account in any matters affecting them. The views of the child should be given due weight according to the age, maturity and capability of the child. (Articles 12 and 13, UN Convention on the Rights of the Child, 1989)

This symbolises a seismic conceptual shift in special education policy since 20 years ago when the foundations for integration were constructed. Now, says the Code of Practice, the groundwork is in place for inclusion. The mainstreaming of children with special education needs is widely supported among educationalists and is considered by parents to be as much a civil liberties issue as an educational one.

The document states that children and young people with special educational needs have a particular understanding of what they need from their schools in order to maximise their educational experience. And this being so, it says that:

> where possible, they should participate in all the decision-making processes that occur in education including the setting

of learning targets and contributing to IEPs, discussion about choice of schools, contributing to the assessment of their needs and to the annual review and transition process.

This is clearly not a tokenistic exercise, but neither is it an easily implemented one. While the guidance says that the climate surrounding the Code of Practice should ensure that children feel confident that their views will be listened to and valued, it goes on to say that

> there is a fine balance between giving the child a voice and encouraging them to make informed decisions and overburdening them with decision-making procedures where they have insufficient experience and knowledge to make appropriate judgements without additional support.

It is an area fraught with difficulties. Not only is there a lack of resolution on the question of who decides whether a child is in a position to make sound, informed decisions about their education – a potential minefield in itself – but there are other complicating factors, too. For instance, children with communication difficulties or with emotional and behaviour problems that may impact on their judgment present challenges to a school that is striving to be participatory for all students. Partnerships with and between other professionals such as educational psychologists, social workers, health workers and therapists will be necessary and of enormous use to schools in helping some children communicate their views. So too will be the use of other communication strategies in the toolbox of special needs educationalists, such as play, art, video, etc.

Schools are expected to seek students' views and record them as part of the statutory annual review process, as well as the IEP and other assessments and reviews, when it is possible to do so. If students wish to communicate with the school through an intermediary, the Code of Practice says that wish should be respected, whether it is through a parent or independent advocate.

The guidance and Toolkit signify progressive thinking about how to involve even the most severely disabled children in the decision-making processes regarding their education and the services they receive to support them in school. But, as Susan Howe, president of NASEN, the National Association for Special Educational Needs, has written, there needs to be more thinking directed into the resourcing for this new multi-agency way of working, and not least of all into training teachers, the majority of whom have no experience of working in this way in inclusive settings. 'Co-ordinating [the various agencies involved] to provide a seamless service is going to require more than good intentions' (Howe, 2001).

What can we learn from research?

The Economic and Social Research Council (ESRC) is funding a major research study on pupil consultation. Schools across the country are working on six research projects over two years. The project summary states: 'From an early age young people are capable of insightful and constructive analysis of their experiences of learning in school and they have a contribution to make to the development of strategies for improving learning and raising achievement'. The project has a network structure in which researchers work with teachers and in support of teachers to open up new dimensions of classroom practice. The project team intends to analyse the growth of interest in student participation by looking at and explaining its development in recent years. They want to explore how children and childhood are described and how this affects how we consult young people. Researchers Rudduck and Flutter (2002) have highlighted an important aspect of consultation: 'Traditionally schools have consulted pupils – often via a school council – about a predictable set of topics (uniform, school meals, and lockers). Over the last few years, however, both the range of topics and the manner of consultation have been extended.' They put forward a much more radical agenda for consulting young people about teaching and learning, school policies and structures, relationships with teachers, pupils and the community.

What's standing in the way?

With exemplary guidance in the form of the SEN Code of Practice, with an international document like the UN Convention on the Rights of the Child, with the Children's and Young People's Unit promoting participation in all areas of young life, with Ofsted inspecting schools for participation, with education for citizenship and the guidance on participation in the Education Act, there is no reason for schools, from the poorest to the most socially and economically advantaged, from those with high numbers of children speaking English as another language to those with a middle class intake, not to be more inclusive, democratic institutions, where students and staff are in partnership and engaged in continuous, mutually respectful dialogue.

But this needs to be approached systematically. For instance, there is no quality control when it comes to school councils. As far back as 1989, the Elton Report *Discipline in Schools* advocated councils but warned of the dangers of not putting the necessary planning and commitment into them:

> We would discourage the creation of token councils. If it becomes clear to pupils that staff are taking no notice of their views, the council is likely to become a liability rather than an asset. Setting up a council that works involves a commitment by staff to listen to what pupils are saying and to take their views seriously. We believe that commitment is worth making. (DES, 1989)

And as we have seen, children and young people have particularly acute receptors when it comes to tokenism and when adults pay lip service to a concept, especially in a school context. But perhaps the most fundamental stumbling block to participation is the culture that can permeate schools that have not gone through a process of self-examination and evaluation of its values and ethos; schools where there is a 'them and us' mentality on the part of staff, where students are tolerated rather than respected, where the notion of discipline takes precedence over respect for the individual, where the pressures to raise achievement compromise the level and tone of interactions between staff and students. As Fielding argues: 'Systems are a necessary but not a sufficient condition for the kinds of changes which advocates of student voice suggest we should implement' (2001, p 106).

Schools also need

> to be more explicitly self-conscious about ensuring that the school council fits in with wider decision-making approaches in the school (e.g. in relation to the Senior Management Team and governors' meetings), as well as with learning goals for students in various groups and as individuals. (Taylor and Johnson, 2002, p 126)

Without a change in the culture of schools – attitudes which create new ways of working with and consulting young people – democratic participation will feel like one more initiative that has been imposed on schools. You can make an argument for it by quoting the UN Convention, the education for citizenship framework, the SEN code of practice, the case for student councils and other frameworks and pledges from the government, but without the commitment to implement it consistently and rigorously, without the ideology to drive it in such a way as to ensure truly inclusive participation, without the creativity and energy to adapt the concepts to the particular needs of your particular students, it will have no meaning and no future.

CHAPTER 4
From theory to practice

The implications for schools of sharing power with students

If children are being equipped to take on the role of active participants and stakeholders, they will by definition be holding the school to account, asserting their right to be listened to and expecting that their views will be taken more seriously than they would be in a more conventional institution. This, as one headteacher who grasped the nettle of participation puts it, is a very different way of operating for most schools:

> How often do pupils have direct dialogue with teachers, managers and leaders in a purposeful, constructive way? What status is afforded to pupil views and issues within school structures? How often do pupil views contribute to the process of change and development in schools? If we were to measure our successes in relation to client satisfaction with, say, the learning environment, preferred styles of learning, range of learning experiences and quality of support and guidance, we would be likely to find some alarming discrepancies between what we perceive and what pupils actually think. (Trafford, B 1997)

And as the Carnegie Young People Initiative report put it:

> ...most schools, for most of the time, along with the society of which they are a part, have systematically underestimated the

> ability of young people to be involved in decisions and have
> clung on to power where it might have been better shared.
> (Cutler, D, Frost, R 2001)

Asking schools to relinquish some control into the hands of children goes against the grain for a number of reasons. For a start, it may appear somewhat rich when schools are filled with professionals who feel themselves to be powerless in their own work and in how their schools are run. Why, they might well ask, should children be given more of a voice when teachers have so little of their own? Fielding makes the point that:

> the development of student voice at the expense or to the
> exclusion of teacher voice is a serious mistake. The latter is the
> necessary condition of the former: staff are unlikely to support
> developments that encourage positive ideals for students which
> thereby expose the poverty of their own participatory arrange-
> ments. (2001, p. 106)

Having to follow a prescribed curriculum in which there is little leeway for creativity, having to take on additional subjects when they are already juggling a punishing timetable as well as time-consuming assessment and having to attend a multitude of meetings hardly makes for a workforce energised by the joys of democratic practice.

There is also the insecurity associated with students taking a more active role in their own learning. To become more independent learners means acquiring the skills to enable them to make choices, to express opinions, take on responsibilities and see them through, to share in planning and decision-making, to negotiate and compromise, to ask appropriate questions and gather relevant information, to argue their case with confidence and commitment. For the teacher, it requires assuming a different role from that which they have been trained in, a transformation from instructor to facilitator, and all that this entails: someone who is there for guidance, discussion and debate. The essence of the change is the relinquishing of control and the willingness to accept students as equal partners in their learning.

But the gains to be had by schools taking this philosophical, pedagogic and psychological plunge are compelling. A research review on school effectiveness succinctly summarises the benefit to students:

> A common finding of effective schools research is that there can be quite substantial gains in effectiveness when the self-esteem of pupils is raised, when they have an active role in the life of the school and when they are given a share of responsibility for their own learning. (Fielding, 2001)

While school effectiveness has become an increasingly contested concept in the last few years, the meaning is clear and when the gains of teachers as well as students are highlighted, the argument for participation becomes more compelling still. One researcher listed them as follows:

- Rules are better kept by staff and students if democratically agreed to in the first place

- Communications in the schools are improved

- There is an increased sense of responsibility as staff and pupils have more control over their own organisation – overcoming the 'them and us' alienation in most schools ... the need to create a sense of belonging

- Decision-making is improved as a range of internal and external interests and opinions is considered Schools are too complex to be run by one person at the top of a simple chain of command... (*ibid*)

To this could be added lower stress levels and enhanced contentment of teachers and students.

As we shall see, these benefits don't necessarily come easy. But with the determination to implement democratic policies and practices, they do come.

How schools are doing it

Schools define participation in different ways and to different degrees. For many, it begins and ends with a student council, which itself is subject to different interpretations and different levels of emphasis in terms of time, energy and rigour. With the government prepared only to suggest that schools run student councils and that schools should allow for participation rather than compelling them to do so, there is plenty of room for lip service and half-baked practice.

But there are outstanding examples of schools to be found in the UK and elsewhere, within the formal education system and outside of it, that are practising democracy with commitment and seriousness. These are institutions which take a holistic approach to participation, involving children in policies, planning and development and suffusing the ethos with a sense of partnership and mutual respect. They do so in the belief that participation isn't merely about giving children a say through student councils, but rather a comprehensive approach to child development within education that benefits everybody working in the school environment.

What follows is a description of some of these exemplary schools. They are discussed in some depth because, in their different ways, they serve as templates which other schools can adapt for themselves.

Sharnbrook Upper School

Louise Raymond, currently deputy headteacher, has been teaching at Sharnbrook Upper School since qualifying fifteen years ago. She was the driving force behind an initiative called 'Students as Researchers,' part of the Economic and Social Research Council's project called 'Consulting pupils about teaching and learning.'

Sharnbrook Upper School and Community College is a large, comprehensive upper school in Bedford with an intake of 1500 students and a Sixth Form of over 500. In the report on the project, Raymond explains how establishing a climate that supports young people has always been one of the school's aims. For over ten years, the school has consulted young people using teacher-designed questionnaires, although she acknowledges that this method uses students as a 'data source.' The frustrations associated with this led the school to involve students in designing the question-naires and developing the questions. 'In this way, students effectively became co-researchers with their teachers, working together to improve their school instead of being just consulted' (Raymond, p 58). Raymond points out that it is crucial that students understand what their role in re-search is and why they need to be involved. She discusses different approaches to working with students that are being used at Sharnbrook Upper School. These include the col-lection of data through questionnaires, small group inter-views, discussions and the move towards allowing students a 'significant voice' through giving them a role as researchers. As part of this project, students were trained from years 9 to 13 in methods of research and evaluation.

> Staff who are involved in the project also attend this training, the crucial issue being that we are forming a new way of working and a new partnership and, as such, it is important that all those taking part in the project fully understand the sensitivities and issues that they will be facing as the enquiry progresses. (Raymond, p 59)

As the project developed, the team focused on involving all groups in the school across the ability range, including some disaffected students.

Annually the project has involved 30 students and four staff, but a much more ambitious and inclusive model is now be-ing developed. Now, each enquiry is located in a curriculum area. This enables a greater number of staff and students to be involved. Areas of enquiry covered include: the use of trainee teachers within the school, gender differences, post-

16 and GCSE choices and the use of ICT. In the school year 2001/2, the enquiry focused on teaching for responsibility, teaching and learning styles and learning using digital technology.

Raymond describes how the culture of the school has not been ready for some of the recommendations that have come out of specific research projects. But the project team has persevered and, slowly, sensitivities have been dismantled and the culture of the schools has changed:

> Ironically, the sensitivities that many staff felt are gradually being broken down by the very virtue of the fact that the students are not, as some would have thought, behaving badly when asked to work in this way. They start thinking about their own learning and engage in their own learning in a far more productive way. In addition, they start to have ownership of their behaviour more generally and in class. (Raymond, p 60-61)

Wolverhampton Grammar School

> Leadership which embraces a participative approach leads to shared vision and goals throughout the school ... Out of this must come almost inevitably unity of purpose: if it does not emerge from dialogue, consensus and compromise, then the participation will have effectively failed. From unity of purpose come collegiality, collaboration and consistency of practice, because it is soon apparent to a teaching staff that mutual support and consistency are vital in the task of teaching if shared goals are to be achieved together: school-based staff development is bound to follow. (Bernard Trafford, headteacher, Wolverhampton Grammar School)

The Wolverhampton Grammar School story, as told by Bernard Trafford in *Participation, Power-sharing and School Improvement*, shows how leadership and commitment from the top can steer a school into the direction of democracy. It also shows how difficult this can be, how important it is to get everyone on board and how he had to learn from his mistakes, some of them painful. The ultimate question is: is it worth it?

When Bernard Trafford took over the headship of this independent school in 1990 after having taught there for nine years, he was determined to bring in a package of new approaches to change the environment of what was a successful school but which had problems of underachievement and disaffection in the sixth form. In his illuminating and instructive account of the process (Trafford, 1997), referred to and quoted at length below, he is disarmingly honest about the triumphs and failures, the agonies and ecstasies, disappointments and joys.

Trafford began laying the groundwork for change by consulting with his staff and the students about what they felt would improve the way the school was run. At the same time, he decided to make the transformation of his school the substance of a doctoral research project, which would also assess the impact of the changes on the school and everyone in it.

Talks with teachers and students illuminated areas of concern, dissatisfaction and frustration with the school. There was also some cynicism about the notion of democratising the school; some students thought that the changes were cosmetic, an exercise to show how good the school was to the outside world. Others suggested that the school council was nothing more than a front erected for the sole purpose of shutting up lippy sixth formers.

But Trafford persisted and brought in a rash of innovations, some on the recommendation of children and teachers, others based on his own ideas of how to create an open, trusting climate. Throughout this process, he solicited feedback and observations from staff and students in group interviews. Perhaps one of the most positive of the early comments he received was from a group of Year 11 students who said that '*ability to question authority is...the greatest advance in a democratic society and this has to some extent been seen in the school*'. (*ibid*)

It was important for Trafford and everybody concerned that the sincerity of his efforts to democratise the school was accepted. Moreover, it was crucial that these innovations were sustained. As one group of students told him:

> Many ideas have been put into place with great sincerity and enthusiasm on the part of all the staff. However...once these ideas are put in place there is a lack of commitment on the part of both pupils and staff to see them through. (*ibid*)

Starting a student council from scratch

As you would expect, the student council was a focal point for development. There hadn't been one at the school before and although there was some scepticism from the outset of the kind referred to above, participants took the council very seriously. It is run by students and is organised entirely by them. Representatives from years 7-11 instituted a system whereby they met directly with the head and their heads of year to discuss particular matters of concern raised at the student council meetings, which ranged widely, from the paucity of lockers to bullying. Students had no lack of grievances, suggestions and demands for improvements, some of which were more feasible than others. There were different reasons for this: some demands were not possible because of lack of space or money, others because of resistance on the part of teachers and administrators to the notion of change coming from the students rather than themselves. A measure of the honesty of Trafford's account in his book is his admission that the slow pace of change was and is still a major issue for and about the student council.

Although the council remains criticised by some students, Bernard Trafford believes that it is valued by the student body as a whole.

Its symbolic importance to the students as the visible manifestation of their empowerment is enormous – greater, indeed, than I ever expected – but is equalled by its practical value to them as a tool which they are eager – again, to an extent that has surprised me – to use productively. Its shortcomings symbolise, always vividly and sometimes painfully, how far there is still to go if the process of empowerment is to be successful (whatever that might mean, since empowerment is arguably a journey without a specific end. (*ibid*)

The role of teachers

While the students had a council to symbolise their role in the democratisation of Wolverhampton Grammar, the teachers had no formal body, no tangible instrument, to show for the changes that impacted on them. However, teachers' role in democratising the school has been proactive. Heads of department, for example, decided that the school's traditional requirement of students having to achieve an A grade in a subject to be able to continue with it at A level should be removed. They regarded it as a rights issue – that a student should be able to study for an A level, if that's what they choose to do and even if they fail in the process. It was, reflects Trafford,

probably the first time that a staff discussion of policy centred on a question of rights for students rather than on the practicalities or pragmatism of school operation. (*ibid*)

Teachers' part in the process has been pivotal, particularly as the rights and demands of students have increased. While sometimes the teachers' position has been in opposition to students' over-reaching demands – such as refusing the student council's request to sit in on heads of department meetings – it has evolved into a culture that by and large takes students' suggestions seriously and deals with them respectfully.

When rights go wrong: the small matter of boundaries

It appears that in the new regime, the line between rights and responsibilities was not clearly drawn. So it came to pass that many students in the sixth form overstepped the line between outspokenness to rudeness, questioning teachers incessantly to catch them out and show them up and commandeering any opportunity in meetings or class to talk about their own problems rather than stick to the matter at hand. It became clear to Bernard Trafford that there was something missing in his model of a democratic school: discipline. But how do you introduce it when at the same time you're developing a liberal, student-centred climate of openness, trust and participation? And how do you instil it when an environment has been newly established in which some students believe that they are entitled to get what they want?

Because ground-rules were not laid from the beginning in a way that had a sustained impact, Trafford found himself sending memos to the sixth form admonishing them that 'freedom brings with it the obligation to do so with courtesy.' But it was clearly not an ideal way of dealing with the situation and should have been pre-empted through discussions and policies rather than dealt with on the hoof.

That experience provides a salutary lesson about the complexities, indeed the highs and lows, of democratising schools and particularly about the importance of laying foundations and clarifying boundaries from the outset.

The impact of participation on relations between the head and teaching staff

Empowering students to make decisions and express their views by definition affects everyone in the school and the relationships within the hierarchical structure. Increased rights for students meant, for some teachers, a sense that their own rights were being eroded. Said one: 'I don't feel I have any more input or say than the kids have, though I should have'.

Trafford realised early on that the spirit of openness, consultation and collegiality among staff was something that required nurturing and time. Staff meetings were one thing, but a different forum, he felt, was necessary to enable staff who felt they had no way of putting forward their views to do so. To that end, he set up a think tank, comprised of ten teachers, who came up with a mission statement for the school reflecting its philosophy.

Measuring school improvement through democracy

What does the school gain, apart from a feel-good sense of bringing in new ways of working? Does it actually impact positively? And how do you measure that impact?

To try to answer these questions, Trafford devised questionnaires for students, teachers and parents and conducted interviews with a random sample of the three groups over a period of two years. The general view among them was that the process of democratisation had been successful. But there was no consensus. While some students spoke of a friendlier atmosphere, a better attitude among teachers, less racism and bullying, others criticised the lack of coherence and consistency. A Year 11 student said:

> ...an atmosphere of 'us and them' has been created as students have realised that they can't have complete power that was at first seemingly promised.

For their part, teachers said that staff and students were happier, that there was more of a feeling of it being 'our school', that there were more possibilities for experimentation and they believed most students felt they are listened to by most members of staff.

One teacher warned that since 'democracy is a journey, not a destination, it will run into problems. For example, if democracy is incremental, sooner or later those steps will hit walls'.

Many parents applauded the fact that the school was more student-centred than before and more relaxed, enthusiastic and positive; a place where students felt empowered and valued. However, some parents concluded that democratising the school was actually a negative development because of what they saw as the causal link between giving children more of a voice and bad behaviour. There was also clearly a mismatch for some students between the open culture at school, where they were encouraged to speak their minds, and a more authoritarian home environment.

Evaluating improvement in terms of exam results, the school collated figures for GCSE and A levels from two years before the school was democratised to six years after. There was an incremental rise in scores, in spite of some year groups being less academically able than others.

Bernard Trafford concludes that the evidence from staff, students and parents, together with the exam data, proves that 'the process of democratisation has led unambiguously to school improvement'. He admits that sharing power within a school takes courage and that his school, being independent, is not subject to new government initiatives and resourcing constraints that maintained schools face. But what his school had to face, like all schools of all complexions, were the internal hurdles. All teachers had to struggle with letting go of the authority that they had previously enjoyed. Both teachers and students had to learn on their feet new skills that would enable them to negotiate and compromise. A new style of protocol had to be learned by students, one which allowed them to communicate their views and demands in a way that was non-confrontational and measured. And everyone had to learn patience: that Rome wasn't built in a day, that democracy is a process, that change doesn't happen overnight, over a term or sometimes even over a year.

In other words, there are a good many lessons to be learned that take time, expertise and reflection. And there are a lot of object lessons to take away from Bernard Trafford's chronicle.

Highfield Primary School

Once there was a school with lots of problems.
There were fights and rows.
Some people broke things, they messed about in class
And did not listen to the teachers.

School was not always a happy place to be.
Sometimes we did not feel safe.
This book is about how we changed our school.
Everyone had to help, not just the few people at the top.
We could only succeed by working together.
(Highfield Junior School, 1997)

While it's one thing to institute democratic policies and practice in a secondary school, bringing these changes to a primary school is another matter. The scale may be smaller, the bureaucracy less labyrinthine and staff perhaps more attuned to the principles, but the risks and labour intensiveness of giving five year old children the skills they need to express their views shouldn't on any account be minimised.

Highfield Primary, or Juniors as it was before its recent amalgamation, is as democratic a primary school as you're likely to see anywhere. It was in the early 1990s that the school underwent a transformation that has made it legendary among citizenship and participation cognoscenti and has been chronicled, like Wolverhampton Grammar's experiences, in a book written jointly by staff, parents and children entitled *Changing our school: promoting positive behaviour*. The title is deceptively simple. What was promoted by changing the school was not just positive behaviour but children's awakening to their own potential, in both the present and the future. Quite simply, the sky became the limit for them in the ways they felt they could positively impact on their school.

But it's necessary to know the genesis of the change at High-field Primary to put it into context. Unlike Bernard Trafford's independent grammar school, the Plymouth primary was victim to the fall-out of the social and economic deteriora-tion that surrounded it. When former headteacher Lorna Farrington first took over at Highfield Juniors, it quickly be-came clear to her that the school was beleaguered by bad behaviour and anti-social attitudes. Set on a notoriously problematic estate in Plymouth, the school was known for widescale bullying, foul language and aggressive parents.

A veteran of special needs teaching in inner city schools, Farrington saw the writing on the wall and realised that a rigorously applied, multi-tiered package of strategies was necessary if the school ethos was to improve. She and her staff developed a range of innovations, including a be-haviour management programme, school council, peer mediation and circle time, among other things. But she took pains to point out in an interview with me in 1998 that these measures weren't pulled out of her suitcase the minute she set foot over the threshold.

> I didn't come here to impose my philosophy on the school. It was the school that engendered a philosophical response that works. Everything that we have done has been informed by what staff and children have to say. (*ibid*)

Early on in the transformation of the school, she was both gratified and taken aback when, during a review of some of the early methodologies that had been introduced, her students told her straight:

> We like this new system but we'll always do things to irritate you because we don't like adults telling us what to do. (*ibid*)

She came back at them with a challenge: to make the school a democracy, with students as the citizens who share in the decision-making. It was the catalyst that would change the role of children at the school, not only giving them a say in how the school is run but giving them the responsibility to carry out the measures they believe would improve things. At Highfield Primary, children from age five are seen very much as partners in their academic, social and emotional education.

Circle time provides the foundation for the democratic process by giving children the social and communication skills they require to make their views heard in other contexts, such as the school council. While circle time has as many different versions as practitioners, at Highfield Primary there is a set procedure for it, firmly anchored in the spirit of democratic practice, with set rules to ensure that everyone has the right to express their views openly but without this causing hurt to others.

Children are encouraged to talk about their feelings and issues that are important to them and problems that need to be sorted out between pupils or pupils and staff, as they do in circle times everywhere, but it is more than that. In the process they are learning, in the words of Lorna Farrington, that 'they have the right to have a say – but not the right to be right'. Ground rules that are repeated at the beginning of every circle time session like a mantra ensure that children understand that honesty is not a licence to be unkind or hurtful. They learn the skill of communicating in a straightforward, factual way.

It's also a forum for making decisions; children decide and negotiate their own rules for their class and for playground behaviour. So it is both a traditional circle time for building self-esteem through set activities and dealing with conflicts and niggles and it's also a time for setting boundaries and making decisions as a group.

One strategy that is sometimes employed is confronting a problem with a particular child from another class by having them join the circle time of the complainant's class, with the teacher mediating. A class teacher who uses this method explains it like this:

> When I say to teachers at other schools that quite often we have the person who's being a problem sit in our circle and the children tell them how they feel, some other teachers are horrified. But we do it in such a supportive way: tell the child you like them but not the behaviour they have chosen. In some other schools, they seem to be afraid to hand over the problem for the children to deal with. It's as if they want to wrap children in cotton wool and never let them put another child on the spot and say 'look, we're not happy with your behaviour. What are we going to do about it together?' Other teachers might tell a story and say 'what would happen if...? Let's pretend that...' but it's not real. We're more direct and tackle it as a team. It's much easier for 30 children to watch out for problems than for one teacher.

Behaviour management isn't in the hands of staff at Highfield Primary. The children themselves manage it through a number of schemes that train and give them responsibility for intervening in conflicts between pupils. One of them, Guardian Angels, is a system of peer support for any child who is in difficulties, whether they are being bullied or are involved in anti-social behaviour themselves that they want to change. When they find themselves in a bind, let's say in the playground, Guardian Angels will 'fly to the rescue' to help mediate the problem. They will also help a child who is trying to improve their behaviour, either by suggesting better ways of interacting with other children or intervening when they see warning signals.

Another strategy is Bully Busters, which children and staff devised while working collaboratively on a behaviour policy for the school. It brings alleged bullying incidents out into the open by making bullying an issue for the whole class to deal with. If a child has been bullied, they post a note into the 'bully box', naming the child who had bullied them and having the option of whether to sign it or not. The slip is discussed at circle time in both the alleged bully's class and the class of the person who sent it (slips are colour coded by class so even if they aren't signed, it is clear which class they are sent from). The children look at whether the accusation is fair or not, if it could have happened, whether the accuser might have misconstrued events. They also work out ways of defusing the situation between the two protagonists.

Although potentially awkward, what the system means is that the problem becomes a communal one rather than one in which victim and alleged aggressor make claim and counter-claim in front of the headteacher. And the children are placed in the position of being involved in the process of adjudication and arbitration, rather than sitting back as passive bystanders. It is an exercise in collective responsibility and in using negotiation, compromise and communication skills for all concerned. The irony is that the children decided very early on that bullying isn't really an issue at the school. There are 'just some people who choose the wrong behaviour' and so most of these kinds of incidents are dealt with in circle time.

In a similar vein, there are house captains, who are voted for by each class after making a speech about what they will do if elected. Their job is essentially supporting children, giving advice and counselling when required. They are given training in resolving conflicts fairly and giving informed advice. They work closely with the peer mediators, also trained, who help children in conflict to find a solution to their problems.

Another innovation is that at the beginning of every year, Year 6 children make a list of all the jobs they could realistically take on to assist with the smooth running of the school. After a couple of days' reflection, they write out job descriptions for each job and then those who wish to write letters of application for specific tasks, such as teachers' assistants, mediators, librarians, monitors for various cup- boards, helping newcomers with literacy and numeracy and first aid helpers. There are also house captains who take res- ponsibility for enforcing behaviour policy.

At the nucelus of these measures is the school council, which was set up as an extension of class-based circle time. Each class has two elected reps and before the fortnightly council meetings, each class has a special circle time to decide what they want the reps to take to the meeting and what they can deal with themselves. The reps make notes of what issues the class wants them to raise and then they report back to the class after the meeting. As well as raising these issues at the school council, the representatives discuss at the outset positive things that have happened at the school to set an upbeat tone. Then they go on to raise matters at hand: needs, problems and, finally, the issue of freedoms and respon- sibilities. As one rep, Mandy, puts it:

> If we want a new freedom, we have to talk about what respon- sibilities we will have or what we will give up so that we can have that freedom. (*ibid*)

One example mentioned in *Changing Our School* describes the time the children wanted the freedom to play war games. Although the headteacher was reluctant on ideological grounds, there ensued discussions that led to an agreement that the games would be allowed as long as the children took responsibility for ensuring that no one would be hurt, that they mustn't interfere with other people's games and that everyone had to stay within the school grounds. It was taken to the student council meeting, where it was agreed to try it out. After three days, one of the children got scared and ran home at lunchtime. The children agreed to a ceasefire for two days as a self-imposed sanction and then to resume the games and see how it went. They took the plan to Ms Farring- ton and she agreed. She wrote of the system:

They can decide on any freedom really if it is agreed by the
School's Council. It has to go through a trial period. All the children talk freely at the meetings. Sometimes we meet formally.
Sometimes we meet in my room around a coffee table and I sit
on the floor to help them feel more equal. (*ibid*)

Arguably the most radical, not to say controversial, component of Highfield Primary's approach to democracy is the
involvement of children in staff selection procedures. This
wasn't among the innovations that were first introduced by
Lorna Farrington when she arrived, but rather evolved from a
school council discussion about the need for new staff at
which a child asked if pupils could be involved in the selection process. Once it was clarified that there were no rules to
prevent children from being involved, the children were
brought on board. Preparation for the interviews is done in
circle time, where the class as a whole talks about the kinds of
questions that need to be asked and the sort of answers they
are looking for. Each class chooses one or two from among
them who they think would be good at asking the questions,
and there is a teacher present at the interview who doesn't say
anything. The children's interview of applicants comes before
the teachers' and then they confer. Said Lorna Farrington:

We always take account of the children's views. We listen
simply to what they think each applicant can contribute to school
life. We decide first and then we read out the children's decisions. The children's and the adults' interview panel have
always chosen the same person, except for last time when we
thought two people were the best. They were all very good
candidates but the children said they wanted music and some
sport, and we were influenced by their decision.

If the children's and adults' panel ever disagreed, I think as a
governing body we would have to rethink our choice very carefully to take account of their views. All the candidates are ad-
vised of the children's role in selection of candidates, and they
have all been very positive.

> I didn't like the idea of setting children up in judgment over adults. The aim is for the children to identify what qualities and talents each person can bring to the school. But when the children talk, it becomes clear who they prefer. They always look for someone who is firm and fair. (*ibid*)

For their part, the interviewees are introduced from the very beginning to the unique nature of the school. They are told that the children's interview is an integral part of the process and that their views are taken very seriously in making the decision. They also see for themselves that the children genuinely take their responsibilities to heart, that they plan the order of questions seriously and know what answers will benefit the school as a whole.

One interviewee who got the job said that the children's interview was the most important of the two interviews because of their rigour and that it was also the most inspiring aspect of the day, leaving her in no doubt that she wanted to work in a school that took children so seriously.

The benefits to the school of bringing children on board as active participants have been enormous. Behaviour problems have reduced dramatically because the children have a sense of ownership, having their say in decision making, policy making, etc. Collegiality is a strong characteristic in the school, among both children and staff, because of the collaborative ethos that participation has engendered. What is crystal clear is that children who are given responsibilities and freedoms grow to meet the challenges that they present.

Today, under a new headship, the school has continued to develop and evolve. While under Lorna Farrington, Highfield was a junior school only; the school is now amalgamated and the freedoms and responsibilities, including the school council, are there for the reception children as much as for the juniors. Those elected onto the council are given training to enable them to run it themselves and the school's visionary approach has impacted on other schools, including the local secondary. And under the direction of deputy head Katherine Palmer, who is in charge of citizenship and oversees the whole programme, the school is about to write another book.

Implications for other schools

While the changes that Highfield Primary have undergone in the last twelve years have been radical and all-encompassing, they are eminently replicable for other schools to use as a model.

The fundamental starting point, however, is the most difficult to navigate: having a consensus among staff, parents and children that change is desirable and that the sustained work that needs to drive that change is possible.

As one class teacher commented, everything that takes place at the school is linked together to give it coherence and strength. So the fact that the school instituted assertive discipline as a preliminary measure because otherwise the teachers weren't able to teach was as much to do with teachers' rights to teach as children's rights to learn and to be safe. To ensure that both rights are upheld, children worked with teachers on mutually agreed rules, boundaries and guidelines.

If it is to permeate the climate of the school, student involvement must be seen in such holistic and developmental terms. Having circle time once or twice a week and running a school council is fine, but this alone is not going to change the ethos of a school or necessarily make children feel that they have a real say in their learning and in the life of their school.

What the example of Highfield Primary shows is that democratisation isn't an easy option: it requires reflection, honesty, risk-taking and hard graft, all buttressed by patience, good communication and negotiation skills, time, energy, intellectual, emotional and practical flexibility and enduring commitment. But what it also shows is that when you have the whole school on board working together, it can turn a school around from borderline failing or just good enough to one that allows its students – and staff – to shine.

Acland Burghley Secondary School, London

As we have seen, there are different ways of sharing power and responsibility in a school. Acland Burghley, a popular comprehensive in north London, has developed a student counselling service, run by and for young people, that empowers everyone involved in it. Using a well designed peer counselling model, it builds on the personal strengths, good will and communication skills of its students.

The Acland Burghley Counselling and Peer Support Scheme, known as ABC, was started in 1993. It was a response to a Sheffield University research report that concluded that teenagers prefer speaking about problems to their peers rather than to parents and teachers.

The scheme has evolved over the years. It first started as a mediation service, in which trained student counsellors would facilitate face to face discussions between bullies and their victims. The counsellors were by and large middle class and the programme was seen as being separate from the rest of what went on in the school. But since then, it has developed into a more sophisticated, solution-based therapy service run by and for students. Rather than a traditional psychotherapeutic style of counselling that looks at the causes of the problem, the approach used by ABC student counsellors helps their peers build up their own strengths by devising strategies for coping and finding solutions to their problem that will, in the process, raise and protect their self-esteem. Crucially, it is buttressed by a tough whole school anti-bullying policy.

Says Vavi Hillel, who coordinates the scheme and is deputy head of Year 7:

> We knew we had to concentrate on the whole school culture if this was to be successful. That's been a big task. What you do with the counsellors once they've been trained, how you bridge the gap between them and the whole school community, how you get teachers and non-middle class students involved and how you reach out to kids and get them to come to you – it's all been a challenge.

The ABC team decided that there needed to be a focus on the transition from primary to secondary, to initiate incoming students into the ethos of the scheme. So it set about establishing links with local feeder primaries. Together, Vavi Hillel and the ABC student counsellors devised drama workshops to take into the primaries. The sessions are designed to prepare the younger children for the new climate of secondary school and to show them options for dealing with difficult relationships and bullying. Reassurance is a strong message: if they come against problems, they are told, there are older students they can turn to for help.

> We ask the primary schoolchildren at the workshop if they want to talk to counsellors. There's always a big queue. (Vavi Hillel)

Stuart Henderson, a counsellor who is in Year 10:

> What makes the drama workshops so successful is that they know we're not teachers. There's a respect level, especially with Year 7s.

The primary school visit is followed by another drama workshop on induction day at Acland Burghley that deals with fears, hopes, getting to know each other, school expectations and with acquainting them with the counsellors.

A local primary school headteacher whose school has been involved for several years believes the workshops have been helpful in different and sometimes unexpected ways: by helping to raise children's self-esteem, helping allay anxieties about transferring to secondary school and by promoting citizenship in the school. They have also, she says, had the effect of bringing to the surface parts of children's personalities that had previously not been apparent.

Being behind in their literacy skills is a major contributor to children's behaviour problems when they transfer to secondary school. Those whose reading ages are several years behind their chronological ages struggle to access the curriculum and often act out their frustrations aggressively or through disruptive behaviour. While ABC is clear in the expectations it sets itself, and particularly that peer supporters alone can't be expected to deal with such serious problems, it's founded on the principle that a proactive and preventive approach can help mitigate feelings of unhappiness and isolation.

To this end, children who will need extra help are identified before they come to Acland Burghley, through links with their primary schools and face to face interviews. They are then matched up carefully with student counsellors.

> One boy had been school phobic and had hardly been to primary school. But with the help of a very pretty sixth form girl who started working with him before he started at secondary school, he settled in well and is now in Year 8 and has never missed a day of school. I can't say whether it was ABC or the general atmosphere of the school but what I can say is that without peer counselling, we would have probably lost him and others, too. Preventing problems from happening from the start is worth all the time and energy we put into it. (Vavi Hillel)

As you would expect from such a rigorous approach, the costs in terms of time and money are considerable. The school has set up a special charity to fundraise for the 14 to 16 hours of training attended by the student counsellors, some as young as 12, over an eight week period at a therapy centre in west London. Training takes place out of school hours.

Student counsellors get an additional two hours of training for the drama workshops. At present, there are around 100 students, or one in twelve of the student body, who are trained in counselling skills. In addition, there are students who are involved in delivering ABC but aren't yet trained. For instance, 40 Year 8s who have not gone through the training have been helping to run the drama workshops in primary schools. They will do so because they want to become counsellors, and training is a requirement for taking on that role.

Vavi has been pleasantly surprised by some of the students who have come forward for training: boys and girls from various backgrounds who are quiet, who may have experienced difficulties in adapting to secondary school themselves. Stuart Henderson is one of them:

> Being at this school and being involved in ABC has helped me hugely. I used to be very timid when I first came here. I hardly knew anybody. I've become much more confident since being here and find it easy to work with Year 7s.

Another student counsellor, Annie McBride, is in Year 9 and says that 'you meet lots of people through ABC so you get to know more about your class.' She first got into it last year when she noticed a Year 7 boy with special needs crying inconsolably on his first day of school. Recalls Vavi:

> She showed initiative. She asked me if she could take him downstairs where there are some computers and sat with him and played games until he settled down. By break

time he said he would go back to class as long as she took him. She wasn't part of the scheme at that point. She just knew it was the right thing to do.

There are some schools where children don't want to be seen to be goody-goodies. But ABC has helped to change that attitude at Acland Burghley.

Headteacher Michael Shew agrees.

ABC has played a part not just in raising the profile of bullying but in helping to establish and maintain a culture of respect between students and between students and staff. By local standards, relations here have been good over the last few years. But we're not perfect. The school has had a high level of exclusions in the past but they're dropping. We'll have under 100 fixed term exclusions this year compared with 180 previously. But the prevailing culture is that it's cool to be nice. And to achieve that you need time and commitment – and particularly teachers committed to pastoral care – but of course it's easier just to teach your subject than to put yourself out.

In addition to ABC, there are other initiatives in place to create a caring ethos in the school. To enable sixth formers to know and befriend Year 7s, volunteers go into classes as support teachers. This has yielded fringe benefits. Not only do the youngest and oldest students in the school have the opportunity to get to know each other and form relationships, but where before, Year 7s were getting virtually no learning support in art, music and drama, now they can turn to older students for practical help.

There is also a Circle of Friends programme, run by a sixth former who helps decide who will be in it. This is a methodology first developed in Canada in which a small group of children volunteer to support and befriend a classmate who is experiencing social isolation because of social or behaviour problems. They are led by a teacher trained in the Circle of Friends Approach, who facilitates the group and to whom members of the circle can turn for help. Throughout the day, the members of the circle take it in turns to support the 'focus child' and there are regular meetings between the group and the child being supported to discuss progress. The supported child receives empathy and companionship but also has to be prepared to hear negative feedback when it arises and to seriously attempt to change their behaviour. The emphasis is on showing the focus child that he or she has choices to make about their behaviour and the trick of it is to communicate this in a positive rather than negative way.

The 100 or so primary and secondary schools who have adopted Circle of Friends since it first came to Britain in 1998 report positive results but are careful not to present it as a panacea for all troubled students.

Michael Shew, who became headteacher at Acland Burghley in September 2002, is upbeat about the strides that have been made through ABC and the other programmes that support students' social and emotional needs. But he isn't complacent. He is keen to monitor its progress through independent evaluations and on the basis of its findings, which would include students' perceptions of it, to develop further and possibly expand the work.

Argyle Primary School, London
For some schools, having a predominantly non-English speaking student population living in an area of grinding inner city deprivation would be its defining feature. Staff and management would see themselves as battling against the odds, doing the best they can but in the belief that there's only so much that's possible when faced with so many problems.

But for this red bricked Victorian school, located at spitting distance from King's Cross station, the sky's the limit. Within its walls, the children, 88 per cent of whom come from poor Bangladeshi families and another few who are asylum seekers, deserve the very best and the school makes sure they get it. If there is a single defining feature of Argyle, it's the commitment to giving children a voice.

The teachers we're talking about aren't delusional Pollyannas. Headteacher Laura Wynne and her team are seasoned professionals at the rough end of spectrum, because it doesn't get much rougher than this neighbourhood. Its transient population, grinding poverty and the ubiquitous presence of prostitutes, drug addicts and the detritus they leave behind have made this area notorious.

But if anything, the grottiness of the world outside the school fuels the determined idealism of those within. Says Laura:

> We know that racism exists, that socio-economic hardship is ever-present in the lives of our families. But in spite of all that, we know that our children can contribute tremendously to society and that they can make a difference to the world in which they live. We have a moral imperative to drive the children hard, to raise their expectations of themselves and to give them access to the wider world... We're here to open doors, to broaden their thinking. (Laura Wynne, headteacher)

One of the guiding principles of the school is open and honest dialogue with the children and each other. There is an emphasis on teachers speaking to each other and the children with respect. It is expected that they will use eye contact, that they will integrate common pleasantries like *please* and *thank you* and *good morning* into their dealings with children, that they will ask how children are and listen to them if they seem upset and that they will have an open-door, welcoming approach to children, parents and each other. Teachers are there as much to be models of good social behaviour as to teach subjects, the staff at Argyle believe.

That is why in their induction, new teachers are versed in the standards of social modelling they are expected to uphold.

But the ethos of the school goes way beyond good manners. Civility is high on the agenda but so too is open, honest and vibrant dialogue in which children are expected to express their thoughts and feelings.

> Many schools do circle time. It gives children turns to have a grumble. We've chosen not to but we're bold in tackling issues like bullying, racism, sexism and children coming in and saying 'my teacher makes me unhappy.' We listen to them and create dialogues. Some teachers find that hard, but we make it clear that what children say comes first and will be taken seriously. (Laura Wynne)

Walking through the corridors of Argyle School during lessons, you don't have to listen hard to realise that this is a different kind of school. Silence isn't a virtue here, which is just as well, since there isn't much. Teachers' voices are punctuated by those of individual children asking questions, contributing their views. It's orderly and calm and very lively all at the same time.

> We encourage children to be inquisitive learners, to question what they're learning rather than passively take things in. Having children constantly questioning you can be a challenge and again, some teachers can find it a problem. We find that it's particularly challenging for those recruited from other countries where there is a more traditional teacher/child relationship, where silence is expected in the classroom.

Social development work is a priority at the school. Through EMAG – the provision for children with English as an additional language – children are evaluated to assess what their needs are beyond the curriculum. Social behaviour, the ability to cooperate and to communicate are given particular attention. From the first term of the first year, the PSHE curriculum focuses on how children can get their message across, how they can make their voice heard in the classroom and how to express their feelings most effectively.

Buttressing the PSHE work is a multi-pronged approach to making children feel sufficiently secure and safe to communicate their thoughts and feelings. A scheme called Playground Friends teams Key Stage 1 children with buddies in Key Stage 2. The older children are trained in how to support the younger ones, empowering them to open up and talk.

Another prong in the drive to give children a voice at Argyle has been the school's involvement in the Listening to Young Children research project by the Thomas Coram Foundation. It explored the ways in which children's views and experiences can become the focus for reviewing services. The Mosaic approach, as it's called, uses children's own photographs, tours and maps as well as talking to and observing them to gain a deeper understanding of their perspectives on nursery and school. It can be a useful method to use with older children too, particularly those with communication difficulties or for whom English is an additional language.

It was through the work with the Coram Foundation that the school set up Talking Groups, rather like little tea parties, where small groups of children come in to the staff room, have some juice and biscuits and talk informally to a few staff members. It's a simple concept and an effective one in breaking down barriers, allowing staff and children to come together socially as members of the same community.

Interestingly, headteacher Laura Wynne finds that the most effective way of bringing staff and children together is the least contrived and elaborate strategy of all.

> It's by having teachers make themselves available and approachable. Each day, a teacher sits in the dinner hall during lunchtime. Every child knows that they can come and talk to the teacher and that we'll listen and act on any

grievance they come with. That encourages them to be open.

The school council is an essential component in the openness and empowering ethos of the school. The staff and senior management take it seriously and apply rigour to its running. It is seen, among other things, as another opportunity for children to develop their speaking and listening skills, and not least of all their ability to formulate and state their opinions. The formal, chaired structure enables everyone present to participate, and it is understood that that is what is expected of them.

But as everyone who has ever run a school council knows, things don't always work out as planned. As Laura Wynne admits:

> Democracy can be a tricky thing. I'm careful to avoid the loudest, most popular children leading the council, as they often can't represent others and just put forward their own views. We've had a situation like that recently – someone who was voted in as chair because of being the best footballer in the school. But it's developed from a potentially difficult situation to a positive one. While he tends to dominate things in other contexts, he's struggled hard to keep his own opinions to one side while he chairs meetings. He's growing through the experience and is developing empathy and an ability to let others speak and keep quiet himself.

Children who prefer not to be involved in the school council have their views heard on particular issues, too. Pupil statisfacation surveys conducted on a yearly basis canvass opinions on a range of subjects, including what they think of the literacy hour and what improvements they would like to see in their school. Children volunteer to analyse the survey and then report their findings back to the rest of the school at an assembly. There is an expectation that the school will address the issues through dialogue in assemblies and through action and the school is held to account if it falls short. Recently, in response to the children's stated desire in the survey for better books in the school library, the budget was adjusted and new and 'better' books bought. The same thing happened when children said they wanted school uniforms. Today, they're as smart as 'posh kids' in their navy sweatshirts and clearly proud of their cool Argyle style.

And finally, parents are an essential ingredient in the whole picture of giving children confidence and a sense of owner-ship in the school. The predominately Bangladeshi families as well as the Somalis and asylum seekers from the four corners of the world are by and large isolated and reticent about venturing out into London. In a bid to help them break through their isolation and to see the educational and social benefits of outings for them and their children, the school invites families to come on the little and big trips that they undertake with the children. It may be just up the road to the British Library or British Museum or it could be to Chessing-ton Zoo. The important thing is that they are learning the ropes of public transport, having their horizons expanded to take in the wonders of what their local community and the rest of London has to offer and, most crucially, are able to understand the ways they can engage their children in dialogue and discussion by observing the teachers' inter-actions with them.

Explains Laura:

> Many people – not just non-English speakers – need guidance on how to interact creatively with their chil-dren. So we invite them to walk with us to the British Library plaza and we'll ask them, 'what can we do here with the children?' It's helping parents to see the oppor-tunities for talk and expanding learning right here on our doorstep.

It's the holistic approach to empowering the children of Argyle School that is so inspiring. It would be so much easier – and so much more beneficial for their league table standing – for Laura Wynne and her dedicated team to focus on literacy and numeracy and not to get involved in professionally run dance projects that help refugee children to express their experiences of transition and loss. It would be so much more straightforward to run an ordinary breakfast club rather than integrate drama work into it to help quieter children come out of themselves. It would be so much less time consuming to not have to take children's views on what to do about blocked toilets and graffiti into account.

But then Argyle would be a very different place. In the ten years since Laura Wynne came to the school as deputy head and her predecessor Usha Sahni took up the headship, there has not been a single exclusion. For an inner city school with all the social, economic and communication problems imaginable, that's quite an achievement. For Laura, it's the only way.

> You have to keep talking up the positive, talking up the children, getting them out into the community, getting them singing in a choir, getting them uniforms if they feel it will give them a sense of identity and pride. We're rigorous in our love for our children.

Young Women's Leadership Charter School of Chicago
Set in a building designed by Bauhaus architect Mies van der Rohe on the campus of the Illinois Institute of Technology in the city of Chicago is a school that represents a unique social experiment. Inspired by the Young Women's Leadership School of East Harlem, New York, the Young Women's Leadership Charter School is the only girls' public (state) school in Chicago and one of only four in the entire country. It is also the only charter school in the city specialising in maths, science and technology. And it is a small school of

less than 400, part of Chicago's trailblazing Small Schools System. The three factors are closely interlinked.

The philosophy underpinning the school is that African American girls living in the run-down, poverty and crime stricken south side of the city need a safe, nurturing but challenging environment in which they can learn subjects at which girls traditionally underachieve; and on from there, a launching pad for careers in which women are under-represented. So the school offers girls an education they would normally only get in a private school: an academically demanding curriculum presented in a safe, secure setting. Says principal Margaret Small: 'Our mission is to support the emerging intellectual curiosity of young women. We want these girls to learn to think of themselves as active agents of their own lives.'

The curriculum is rigorously designed and executed at a level indistinguishable from private schools that prepare students for university. New computers in every classroom support and complement each subject, as you would expect in a specialist technology, science and maths school. Aspirations are high and encouragement is in the very ether of the school, as it needs to be when 70% of students are on free school meals and a significant proportion are the first generation in their families aiming for college.

The high academic level at which the teaching is pitched is complemented by project work designed to make the subjects relevant to students' lives. Far from being an academic hothouse, the school is a laboratory in which students explore, learning for themselves as well as receiving challenging instruction, and making choices every step of the way.

Students decide what subjects they wish to pursue in their project work. Humanities offers a huge scope for students to set their agenda. For instance, in their humanities module on the Harlem Renaissance, one class voted to research the under-acknowledged achievements of women during that vibrant period of African American history. In a module called Project Citizen, three classes described their neighbourhoods: what they are like and how they would like them to be. They identified the problems they wanted to focus on and spent two months researching the social realities of those problems In a chilling reflection of their day to day lives outside of school, one group chose to concentrate on rape and sexual harassment.

Eva, a 14 year old who showed me around the school, pointed out a vividly painted mural on the wall depicting the twin towers. 'This area had been blank and looked empty so we asked the permission of the teachers to make it into a September 11th commemoration area.' That section of corridor has now become a focal point in the school, with many other students making their contributions to it in drawings, paintings and poetry.

A fundamental factor in the engine driving student participation at the school and particularly in the way they experience the curriculum is its size. While the classroom size of around 25 students is about the same as the averge British comprehensive, it is the overall student population of the school that appears to make a significant difference in the way students and teachers feel and operate within it. Recent research conducted by the Bank Street College of New York (Small Schools, Great Strides, 2001) shows that students who attend small schools have lower truancy and dropout rates, have a stronger attachment to their schools, demonstrate a higher degree of persistence in their studies and perform better academically than peers in larger schools.

At least as interesting as the measurable advantages of smaller schools are the qualitative differences between them and larger schools. Small schools appear to ameliorate the feelings of isolation and alienation that are often triggers for the kinds of violence that are found in large schools of 1,000 students or more. The researchers found that because of the increased sense of identity and community that comes with knowing and being known by every teacher and peer in a small school, violence and aggressive behaviour is far less frequent. Conflict management is easier to facilitate and the values of democratic citizenship define school ethos. Looking at the Bank Street research, you can't help but wonder whether the 1999 massacre at Columbine High School in Colorado (in which two disaffected students killed twelve students and a teacher before turning their guns on themselves) would ever have happened if the young, troubled gunmen had gone to a school every day where there was a scaled down, more personalised and nurturing environment.

Because everyone knows each other in small schools, teachers feel more secure and fulfilled in their jobs and in their relations with their students, too. They also report a heightened degree of professional cohesion with their colleagues. This is reflected in the ways that they report a more active engagement with professional development and ploughing more energy into creating focused learning environments for their students, including more diverse teaching strategies to better meet students' needs. Most noteworthy in light of the present teachers' shortage crisis on both sides of the Atlantic, they say that working in small schools reinvigorates them and intensifies their commitment to teaching.

In addition, the increased involvement of parents and community members in small schools paves the way for easier communication and more comfortable relations between the school and those it serves.

While these findings make the principle of small schools eminently attractive, the Bank Street research takes pains to point out that merely paring down the size of a school is not a panacea to the social, economic and academic problems that students bring in with them. Without the practical and ideological support of Chicago's chief education officer and business and community partners, small schools such as Young Women's Leadership cannot and will not survive. A number of small schools in Chicago had to close down within two years of opening because of the lack of strong management structures and whole school cohesion. This points to the necessity of setting aside time and space from the beginning for teachers and senior management to carefully discuss and plan the vision and mission of the school and continually refer to them in their day to day work. It is only through this developmental way of working that a strong team can be built, that mutual understandings can be created, that realistic and enduring structures and regulations can be designed.

The research also pointed to evidence suggesting that the most successful small schools seek out data on best pedagogic practice and integrate it in their own teaching rather than relying on trends.

All these initiatives and approaches, say the researchers, count for little unless and until there is a change of culture in the systems that are there to support them. An education authority or school district that has been constructed to run average or large sized schools will find it difficult if not impossible to acculturate to scaled down schools. Acknowledging this cultural divide, the Chicago Public School System, which is led by a chief education officer so committed to small schools that he has pledged that no new school will contain more than 600 students, has created a separate department that will oversee the 20 small schools being set up in the next five years.

Young Women's Leadership School was awarded a charter by the Chicago Public School System in 2000, which allows it to deliver the curriculum of its choice in the way it chooses to, without having to conform to the rules and regulations of other public schools. In exchange, it has to meet set achievement targets by a certain time. If it doesn't, its charter is revoked and it must close.

Principal Margaret Small works to ensure that the school achieves what it has set out to do and is determined, in her words, to:

> help teachers learn to deal with the challenges of supporting students' voices and sharing authority in the classroom while at the same time retaining their authority. I'm constantly looking at how I can be supportive of teachers while keeping students at the centre of their education. Of course we have limits on what we can do because of our class sizes, which are more or less average for high schools. But we have a pretty young faculty, all of whom are attracted to our mission. And the culture of the school, among other things, creates a sense of ownership and minimises alienation on the part of everybody.

It is an interesting juggling act that Young Women's Leadership has taken upon itself, with three different but interlinked ideologies:

- it is a small school, committed to an individualised, supportive, community-style environment

- it is an all girls' school, committed to providing a challenging, aspirational curriculum within an empowering and democratic framework

- it is a charter school, committed to providing a service that is distinctive and not hidebound by public school system regulations

What it all means so far, according to Ms Small, is that:

> We're about winning our students over to want to take responsibility for their own learning. They have a clear perspective on what they are learning and not learning,

on what their strengths and weaknesses are and on what's important, what's not important – and why.

Participation and students with special educational needs

As previously discussed, students with special educational needs are often the outsiders when it comes to even the most basic forms of democratic practice, for a variety of reasons. The Ofsted Review (1999) *The SEN Code of Practice: Three Years On* found that while the involvement of parents vis-a-vis Individual Education Plans had risen as a result of the introduction of the Code of Practice, by and large students remained outside the process. But it is also true that special schools traditionally have had a more individualised approach to students for obvious reasons of scale and need.

In 1999, seven special schools, some residential, some day schools, came together to collaborate on an action research project that challenges traditional beliefs about the role of children with special needs in their schools. The headteacher of one of the schools involved, the Edith Borthwick School, gave the rationale for the project when it was first introduced at an Essex special schools in 1995:

> ...too many students within the special school sector, and more widely in the mainstream sector, experience narrow approaches to learning and teaching, where their own preferred learning styles are largely ignored. Disaffection and poor self-esteem result from consistent mismatch between preferred and prescribed styles. Disaffection and poor self-esteem lead to anti-social and negative behaviours, which in turn lead to more challenging behaviours and, ultimately, exclusion. (Jelly *et.al.*, 2000)

Supported by Essex education authority, they designed a model that would increase student autonomy in their own learning on a number of different levels. The *Involving Pupils* project was built around engaging students in the various stages of their progress and in participating in the institutional development of their schools. They were facilitated to this end by being taught skills that would develop their critical thinking, problem solving and communication capabilities.

Each school developed their own strategies and methodologies, depending on the needs of their diverse student populations, who ranged from children with emotional and behaviour difficulties to those with severe physical disabilities. They were assisted by two project leaders who coordinated the project, in addition to the headteacher of that particular school and an LEA representative. Evaluation and training were also embedded in the project.

The schools identified focal points on which the work would need to be concentrated. Among them were pupils' involvement in individual education plans, in tracking targets and self-assessment, in the annual review process and the development of school councils to give students a forum for influencing policy and practice.

Pupils' involvement in their assessment
There is a growing body of thought that reflects the underlying principle of the project: that children with special educational needs should be involved, when possible, in assessing their schooling experience. In the words of the *Code of Practice* itself

> Involving children in tracking their own progress within a programme designed to meet their particular learning or behavioural difficulty can contribute to an improved self-image and greater self-confidence. (*ibid*)

Educational psychologists and SEN teachers including Gersch (Gersch, 1996) and Galloway *et al* (Galloway, 1994) have observed and written about how crucial a role student involvement is, not only in the process of identifying special needs but also in their empowerment in the learning process. When they are consulted about their needs, they are likely to feel more in control and see the possibilities of progression. By having their views solicited, listened to and valued, whether it's by an adult staff member or peer, these children, many of whom have little say elsewhere in their lives, can experience a surge of self-esteem and consequently a more positive attitude towards their schooling.

One example, taken from *Involving Pupils in Practice*, highlights the wisdom of involving students in the review process. Anna, a Year 8 girl at Cedar Hall, a school for 5-16 year olds with moderate learning difficulties, was considered by the staff to be ready for part-time reintegration into mainstream school. Her academic progress was what had convinced teachers that she could successfully do this. But when the issue was raised at the one to one tutorial that precedes the Annual Review, Anna made it clear that she wasn't prepared to try to go back to mainstream at that time. When her views were taken back to the staff, although they hadn't picked it up in the initial assessment, they agreed on reflection that Anna was right in holding back: her low self-esteem and poor self-confidence would have worked against her in a bigger, less supportive environment. They respected her views and reassessed her situation, setting targets that would boost her confidence and independence, including giving her the responsibility of helping younger children learn to swim. A year later, she was more positive and able to look forward to reintegration as a realistic option.

The whole business of involving students with their learning has to be about much more than just coming to meetings or tutorials if it is to be a meaningful process. When it's taken seriously, it demands sensitivity and reflection on the part of staff and perhaps access to counselling for some students.

Thinking skills
Alongside using circle time and school councils to air students' views on policy and curriculum development issues, it was decided to include a thinking skills component

in the *Involving Pupils* project as a means of empowering children. Each school had a different way of approaching it. The Longview Unit, a short-term adolescent psychiatric unit offering multi-disciplinary, specialist assessment and treatment, developed an approach that included Skills for Adolescence. Among other themes, it focuses on building confidence through enhanced communication and developing critical thinking skills for decision-making. The approach was chosen for the transferable skills it gave to students, which were particularly useful for those who would be moving back to mainstream. Said one:

> What I am taking away with me from these programmes is the confidence to speak out and say clearly what I really think. This has particularly helped to get me back to school. (Jelly *et al*, 2000)

A continuum of participation

This is a good term to describe the way participation was developed in the project, moving by gradations from low level – gathering students' views in order to inform decisions on school development – through to consultations with students about the need for and nature of change, on to higher level forms of participation that actively engage them in decision-making. As the level of involvement increases, so does the empowerment of the students, including in terms of their relationships with teachers. This is unlikely to be a sudden or necessarily intentional change but, as the schools have found, moving along the continuum becomes a natural process once a culture of listening to pupils has become embedded in the life of a school. (*ibid*)

The very empowerment that the project schools wished to develop presented significant challenges, as all democratic processes do and as all schools who introduce them must be prepared for. At Edith Borthwick School, a questionnaire completed by one year group annually over a three year period as part of their PSHE programme initially yielded unexpectedly negative results for staff. Particularly disturbing was the low self-esteem they found that many students felt, a lack of trust and confidence and students' inability to deal with negative feelings. The results of the questionnaire also indicated student's perceptions of the failures of staff: 64% of students said the work they were given to do was not always appropriate to their ability level; 64% said they were afraid of other people in the school; 32% would rather not be at school; 52% didn't like being told what to do by teaching staff. Three years later, however, there were more positive responses, particularly to the questions reflecting self-esteem and attitude to school.

Most importantly, the action research approach of the project led to systemic changes in the school, which took the views of students seriously. Among the changes that took place as a result of the project, and particularly in response to the widespread social problems students revealed were the establishment of a school-based youth club, a wider range of residential activities and better contact with parents.

Sharpening up student councils

Hayward School, a school for 3-16 year olds with moderate learning difficulties, had a school council that students had identified as ineffective, largely because it was in the hands of a few larger than life boys who had somehow managed to rig elections and didn't take their roles seriously. The council was disbanded and staff and students tried to work out a better election model. They also determined that there needed to be some kind of preparation for the elections and for those who were willing to stand as representatives. So they agreed that tutor groups would receive a module on citizenship as part of the curriculum and would then be balloted for their choice of reps, with the criteria for election made explicit.

To help them in the process of electing the most suitable candidate, time would be allocated to discussing the school council in PSHE classes. In addition, agendas and minutes would be sent to the reps and class tutors and important school council business would feature in assemblies.

When it came to the substance of the council meetings themselves, students were encouraged to discuss all issues by dividing them into either 'dreams' or 'realities', ie, the possibly unachievable aspirations and the changes that were realisable. The proof of effectiveness can be seen in the long list of improvements to the school that have come about thanks to action taken by the council. As well as lobbying for new equipment and environmental improvements like a wildlife garden, vandalism to students' toilets has been reduced as a result of a student rota in operation at breaktimes and conditions in the playground have also improved after staff were asked not to talk to one another during playground duty.

The thinking behind this holistic package is this: to make school democracy meaningful, the concept of democracy has to be deconstructed in a way that allows students an understanding of what the democratic process means. And just as crucially, they need to be given the tools to exercise it. It's a lesson that applies as much to selective schools and comprehensives as it does to special schools.

As some students voted onto one of the school councils in the project put it, the purpose of the council and, it could be argued, the purpose of the entire project, is:

> to voice the opinions of children, the voice of everyone to get things done. It proves that you can be grown up. It's a very good thing. It is giving other people the chance to have their say. (*ibid*)

The lessons to be learnt from the project
The project as a whole has important lessons for all schools. For some of the participating schools, it meant embracing a

significant shift in culture: collaboration between staff and students, changes in curriculum content, restructuring the social organisation. But perhaps most fundamentally, it was a catalyst for a seismic philosophical shift in teachers' thinking about their own roles and responsiblities. As one teacher put it:

> I never used to think about what pupils might want out of my training. It was always a personal viewpoint – a kind of self-centred approach. The project has made me rethink all of that. Pupils told us what they needed us to be able to do, and that's how I view my training needs from now on. (*ibid*)

That it was worthwhile for the schools as a whole is clear. The evaluations, carried out by the two project leaders, Mike Jelly, headteacher at Edith Borthwick School and Alan Fuller, senior education psychologist at Essex LEA and Richard Byers from the University of Cambridge School of Education, show the wide-ranging benefits to students, teachers and their schools as a whole. Here are some of the key findings.

Effects on students
- Enhanced assertiveness and confidence to express their views, articulate their needs and share their skills. Examples: two students from one of the project schools helped deliver an LEA run workshop on thinking skills for teaching staff. Another gave a powerpoint presentation to professionals at a conference on a voluntary scheme his school was running.

- A proactive, can-do approach to problems. Example: at a school where the counsellor was over-stretched, some Year 10 pupils suggested setting up a peer run listening service.

- The development of effective school councils and the improvement of existing ones. Example: the evaluation found that schools expressed an enhanced sense of purpose within the council, as witnessed by students' more focused decision-making, greater independence, ideas about how to develop the council further and a more realistic approach about how to effect change in the school.

- Through expressing their teaching preferences and thereby getting more individualised and flexible teaching styles and support, children reintegrated more easily into mainstream provision.

- Students see their individual education plans as an important element in meeting their needs.

- Targets are set collaboratively with teachers, giving students a sense of ownership over them instead of the feeling that the targets are being imposed upon them.

- The focused attention on students led to fewer incidents of difficult behaviour; staff used the opportunity of one to one tutorials on target setting to offer students techniques for coping with anger, frustration, etc.

Effects on staff

- The project gave staff a framework within which to reflect on their own practice in a way that wasn't possible before.

- It gave them the freedom to try new strategies and methodologies.

- Staff have developed greater confidence and trust in students and vice versa.

- They have gained skills in target setting and helping students to achieve their targets.

- Their skills in communication and planning, coordination, group structuring and monitoring have improved through the process of staff and personal development that being involved in the project has entailed.

- Opportunities were created for joint planning, team-teaching and collective critical analysis of what they were doing.

- Feedback by students at the end of every day in tutorials illuminated to teachers what did work and what didn't and led to adjustments and sometimes major changes in their teaching approaches.

- A spirit of collaboration and camaraderie amongst staff within and between the project schools and between project coordinators was engendered.

Effects on the curriculum

- For some schools in the project, the project clarified the need for thinking skills to delivered through PSHE.

- For others, it led to the realisation that priority in the curriculum should be given to developing social skills and self-esteem, leading to a reassessment of the pastoral curriculum and staff training.

- At another school, an outreach programme was developed on the basis of the needs highlighted in the project.

- Improvements to the assessment process have been made in some of the participating schools.

- A re-examination of the curriculum has led, at one school, to the content being more geared to the skills students need to reintegrate into mainstream.

- Schools reported improved data management and greater efficiency at planning and implementing projects.

Balwearie High School, Kirkcaldy, Scotland

Since devolution, the Scottish Executive and Parliament have taken responsibility for children's and young people's interests with rigour, coherence and commitment. Among other things, the Executive commissioned Save the Children to devise a consultation framework and asked the Centre for the Child and Society to research the efficacy of different methods for consulting young people. It has also set up a Young People's Parliament and a Scotland-wide youth summit in 2000, the latter attended by the entire Scottish cabinet. But the icing on the Scottish cake in terms of school democracy has been a watershed piece of legislation – the Standards in Scotland's Schools Act 2000 – that legally requires headteachers and LEAs to involve children and young people in decisions related to their education, taking into account their age and maturity. They now have to listen to what students think and say in matters that affect them in school.

At Balwearie High School, some of the spirit of that legislation is embedded in practice. And unlike the previous schools under discussion, it is a large school by any standards: 1,750 students, including 95 in a special needs unit who attend mainstream classes for some subjects.

Learning and teaching has been a focus of the school in recent years and the student body has been closely involved with this in a number of different ways.

The most traditional of these routes is through the student council. Within the council, working groups of 'council volunteers' have worked on specific issues. One group dealing with bullying pioneered an anti-bullying campaign which has been successful and high profile within the school. The council has also generated elegant, simple solutions to problems it has identified. For instance, council members raised concern at the difficulties of planning for the large amount of homework, revision and assessments they were having to complete at the same time. Senior management took the issue to heart and while it could do nothing about the curriculum deadline schedule, it arranged to provide all students working towards exams with deadline calendars at the beginning of the school year.

Students' views on the curriculum are also sought. A number of carefully designed questionnaires distributed to students throughout the last decade asked them to reflect on a range of issues, including their preferred ways of learning, the resources they found most effective, classwork, homework, study support and tests. Their responses have led to changes in the way they are taught. In response to students' suggestions that they needed more frequent tests to make sure they understood the material, mini tests for knowledge and understanding have been introduced three times during each topic. After chemistry students said that the subject should be made more interesting, teachers made more use of software programmes, powerpoints and videos in their teaching. Due to public demand, more help sheets have been produced, containing lists of keywords and summaries on topics.

Students in S5/6 (equivalent to Key Stage 4) set their own formal targets in collaboration with staff. This is done through dialogue with the subject teacher. While teachers are free to challenge students' selected targets on the basis of previous performance and other realities like time and realistic commitment, the target set is the students': staff are not allowed to impose their view of reasonable targets on the student, even if they feel that it has been set inappropriately high or low. But they are expected to give guidance on how these targets can be achieved and students have the chance to revise their strategy for achieving their goals at the two reviews held with guidance staff between the time targets are set and when they sit exams.

Students in the SEN unit also make their own targets, with guidance from teachers, and are awarded certificates for achievement in the areas of effort, behaviour and relationships. In addition, students rate themselves according to how they match their targets, which are broken down into short term, manageable aspirations.

Those students who are disaffected with school are able to follow an alternative curriculum, customising their own course of studies through a combination of work experience, courses at local further education colleges and a reduced school curriculum, supported by the careers service and mentors.

All students and their parents are given the opportunity to give feedback on their reports as well as suggestions for future action, and the school strives to respond to issues that are raised by students and parents.

As well as self-review and assessment being a standard approach at the school, there are opportunities for peer assessment in Physical Education, in practical work and in English during oral activities.

It is a measure of the school's responsiveness to students' suggestions that when students have expressed requests for after school and lunchtime clubs and classes, teachers have committed their free time to ensuring that these extra curricular and support activities are delivered.

One teacher at the school summed up the impact of this climate of dialogue on the learning that takes place at Balwearie High School:

> The pupils are much better prepared to tackle the challenge of studying in today's combative environment. They have a determination to learn and they show a responsibility for their learning. I saw a biology class which was formed into three groups, each taking a different topic and presenting it to the others, teaching it, as a way of reinforcing the learning. (www.ethosnet.co.uk/case study 22a.htm)

CHAPTER 5

What students want

There is little research in Britain or elsewhere that ex-
plores the gulf between students' perceptions of what
school and education could and should be and the
realities of their school lives.

What we do know is what we can glean from the few surveys
and soundings that have been taken. They make important
reading for all educationalists, not least because of the gulf
that exists in young people's minds between the ideal and
the real.

In an ideal world...
Responses from primary and secondary schoolchildren
around the country to *The Guardian's* 2001 ideal school
competition reveal young people's enthusiasm for discussing their experiences of school, rooted in an inspiring
idealism. This ranges from the positive to the missed opportunities to the injustices and deficits that they feel they have
no recourse to change in their schools.

One of the winners, 15 year old Miriam Grossfeld from Reading, Berkshire, brilliantly articulated the aspirations and disappointments that many young people of different generations have about their school experiences:

In my ideal school, the whole philosophy that dominates schools now will be dropped. It will be somewhere thriving with different personalities and gifts, where these things can be developed and used to help everyone else. We will no longer be treated as herds of an identical animal waiting to be civilised before we are let loose on the world.

We will cease to be thought of as useless vessels waiting in disciplined conditions to be filled with our quota of information, just so we can regurgitate it all in exams so that our school looks good in the league tables.

The winner in the 11-14 category, Maise Monroe, evoked what she admitted is a utopian ideal but one that touches on the complex and interlinked problems of schools in the real world.

If I went to my ideal school I wouldn't wake up and dread the next day, the next week, the next year and the rest of my life ... In my perfect school there would still be rules, but they would guide us, not confine us. Teachers and children would mesh harmoniously. There would be no grading, praise only for working hard and not your mental capability ... Exams would be abolished, people would work together and alone, they would use other people's knowledge to enrich themselves and others would do the same with them. We would discuss our opinions in every lesson ... Teachers and pupils would be equal. In my school the only things they would ban would be unhappiness and pain, no room for lying, revenge and deceit. (*Education Guardian,* June 5 2001)

The competition, run as a follow-up to the 1967 'The School I'd Like' competition by *The Observer*, had distinctive echoes of its forerunner. Children's writer Edward Blishen, who judged both, wrote after the first event:

From all the quarters of the educational scene it comes, this expression of children's longing to take upon themselves some of the burden of deciding what should be learned, how it should be learned.

What is so striking is that those words could have been written today. While so many aspects of western life have changed beyond recognition – science, technology, social structures, the arts – the way schools have been run to date is not appreciably different to the way they were run in 1967. Students still feel invisible and disenfranchised.

A more generalised picture of children's perceptions of school can be seen in a survey based on questionnaires sent to 2,272 seven to 17 year old pupils, in which they cited 'particular lessons' and 'teachers' as the things they liked least about their school. Not as contradictorily as it may first appear, the top two things they liked most about their school were sports/PE and 'particular lessons.' (*Guardian*, 2001) It's hardly rocket science but it is worth being reminded that when a subject is taught well, lessons are exciting, attractive and engaging for students. When they are delivered badly, students down mental tools and switch off or worse, truant.

Refugees
More specific surveys reveal the daily realities of groups whose voices are not often heard. The Horn of Africa Youth Scheme (HAYS), in partnership with Save the Children, ran a peer research project on the educational support needs of 34 young refugees and asylum seekers in an inner London borough, most of whom had arrived in the UK within the last four years. Nearly half had been 'looked after' by social services at some point since arriving here. Although this cohort represents a small proportion of the 50,000-odd young people in London alone who fall into the category of refugee/asylum seeker, it is a rare perspective on the experience of this diverse group in British schools.

What emerged from the survey was that many young refugees, despite placing a high value on education, have a miserable time in British schools. Entering a new school is hard enough for anybody; but these students speak little English, come from countries with very different education systems to ours and many will have experienced emotional distress before and since leaving their home countries. Often living in care or on their own, many feel lonely, depressed and at sea being so far from their families and countries. They feel alienated from the different culture within the school as well as outside it. They are isolated from their peers because of language problems and also because of their differentness: over half suffer racist taunts or bullying by other students.

Language is the obvious stumbling block to inclusion. Said one:

> It was very bad. I couldn't speak English properly. If you're from another country and don't speak well they do not respect you at all.

But even having a bit of English is not enough when schools lack a systematic induction programme for refugee students, backed up by ongoing support. Nearly all those interviewed said they would have found information about the education system here valuable. The assumption that students of all ages will adapt easily to a system that, in these young people's cases, is so different to what they were accustomed to is misconceived. As another student put it:

> It would have been helpful ... to know the system. You don't know what subject you are choosing. You just do what the teachers suggest. Year 10, I didn't know how important it is (to choose options) as I didn't get any advice.

While the majority were positive about the help and support they received from teachers, some spoke of teachers treating them differently to other students and of regarding them generically as refugees without attempting to understand them as individuals.

Almost all were in favour of having other young people in school help them with their English, although they were divided between those who preferred them to be English and those who wanted people from their own background. As well as the practical language support, they spoke of the social benefits and help with getting them orientated in the culture of the school that peers, rather than teachers, could give them. This was particularly important in view of the fact that because of their language difficulties and differentness, they were targets for racist bullying.

The peer researchers who carried out the interviews, and to whom the students disclosed thoughts and feelings that would otherwise not have been aired, concluded their report with recommendations for schools, among which are the following:

- Orientation and induction, including information about the British education system translated into relevant languages, should be made available to all new refugee students. This should include guidance and help on making informed choices about courses, qualifications and career routes.

- Assessment of students' language needs should be carried out and appropriate support provided to match their needs by specially trained teachers and also peer educators.

- Students should be able to choose whether or not teachers are informed that they are refugees.

- Schools should ensure that teachers have background information about students' different home cultures and integrate positive examples of those cultures into lessons.

- There should be a sufficient number of refugee support workers to help students access services, make the right choices for their own future and ease integration into school.

- Young people, both refugees and non-refugees, should be involved in running training workshops for refugees on strategies for dealing with bullying and racism.(Save the Children, 1998)

Girls

An action research project carried out by the London Borough of Newham and its accompanying report entitled *Girls' Voices: are they on the agenda?* (Cruddas *et al*, 2001) sheds light on the school experiences and needs of a sector of the pupil population whose views often go unheard. Teachers in five project schools set up a programme of developmental group work with girls who had been identified as having emotional or behaviour difficulties. Participation in the groups gave the girls an opportunity to explore the relationships between themselves and others, at home and at school. In this protected space they had the freedom to communicate important insights into their own behaviour and, most relevant to this discussion, to describe the things they believed would improve their school experience. It was an opportunity they seized. Their testimony is insightful, moving and eloquent.

Among the things they said they wanted at schools were:

- to be supported by better pastoral systems
- to be listened to
- to be heard above the boys
- to be treated as equals
- to have emotional space
- to have friends
- to share problems with each other

Above all else, they said that to function better in school and at home, they needed to be listened to. They felt that this wasn't happening at school and when they did air their problems they weren't always taken seriously. These are some of their remarks:

'Teachers need to talk to girls like equal human beings.'

'Some teachers don't listen because they think we're young and don't know anything.'

'I think it's sad that we had to have this group just to voice our opinions. Don't teachers realise that we've got opinions?'

'It's the way teachers talk to us. We're not dirt, you know.'

'If you've got problems, they're with you all the time – we need space to deal with them.'

All the girls spoke of not being treated fairly by adults because of their lack of status as young people. They spoke, too, of the lack of 'emotional space' in school life; that their heavy emotional baggage had nowhere to be stashed away in the school environment, that there was no-one to help them resolve their considerable problems or even to acknowledge that they had them.

They expressed the wish that school should support them through formal and informal pastoral work that was flexible and carried out by people with whom they feel comfortable. There were four ways in which this could be achieved:

- Through form tutors, who were identified as the most likely teachers to pick up on problems because of their regular exposure to students. However, because of personality clashes, perceived indifference on the part of the tutors or time constraints, this isn't always a viable option.

- Through PSHE lessons, which some girls felt offered possibilities for group work because of the curriculum content. Again, the attitude and personality of the teacher was a crucial factor in whether PSHE would be effective or not.

- Through subject teachers, useful when problems are to do with work.

- Through professionals not on the school staff. Many of the girls preferred to speak about personal problems to non-teaching staff, based on their experience of the action research groups.

- Counselling agencies from outside should be brought in for girls to have access to during school time, possibly on a drop-in basis. Their availability and descriptions of their services could be made known by posters, in assemblies and during tutor time or PSHE.

Based on the girls' responses, the researchers drew up a set of recommendations, among which were the following:

At LEA level:

• A named person to monitor equal opportunities issues (gender, ethnicity, SEN)

• Promotion of strategies to support emotional literacy to help remove barriers to learning and participation

• Establishment of a forum to coordinate provision of support from statutory and non-statutory agencies

• Development of effective home/school liaison practices

• Staff development to raise awareness of emotional needs of young people in context of inclusion and equal opportunities

At school level:

• Staffing and resources to be reviewed in order to meet emotional needs of girls and all students

• Development of more flexible responses to girls' emotional needs, including informal support networks

• Better understanding of services offered by statutory and non-statutory agencies

• Development of home-school liaison practices

• Raising staff awareness of emotional needs of all young people. Re-evaluating pastoral systems, particularly the role of tutors and training needs

Children and young people with disabilities

Approximately one in 20 children have a disability, representing a wide spectrum of physical, cognitive and sensory impairments, from mild to profound. While the issues they face are diverse, there are certain recurring themes among many children in this category, including social and economic difficulties and social isolation. Probably the single most common denominator between them is the constraints they face when it comes to making their voices heard. While there may be a general, if gradual, trend towards including children in consultation processes related to their education and welfare, those with disabilities remain by and large locked out.

In the section on enabling pupil participation in the DfES' SEN Toolkit (Section 4: *Enabling Pupil Participation* 2001), a model template is set out for schools. The guidance entitled 'To participate in decision-making' says:

> Children need information and support so that they can work towards:
>
> • understanding the importance of information
>
> • expressing their feelings
>
> • participating in discussions
>
> • indicating their choices
>
> Adults need to:
>
> • give information and support
>
> • provide an appropriate and supportive environment
>
> • learn how to listen to the child

Based on the little research that exists on disabled students' perceptions of schools, there is a long way to go before this model is realised. While there are education authorities and schools working towards inclusion, for many others the rhetoric of inclusiveness is hollow.

A qualitative study of the views of various facets of young people with disabilities' lives (Watson and Shakespeare, 2001) offers rare illumination of the way they see the world, and particularly within the parameters of school life, and their place in it. The 165 11 to 16 year olds interviewed had insightful if negative things to say about their experiences. Generally, they expressed their sense of being marginalized and disregarded. They felt that their abilities were under-estimated and their need for dependence on others assumed.

For some of these students, inclusion is nothing more than a nice word. They are aware of being taught mainly by un-qualified special needs assistants in mainstream schools rather than by the class teacher. They have little or no privacy and are spoken about by teachers as if they are not there; even their medical conditions and home lives are discussed by teachers in front of other students. One child is quoted as saying, 'It may be hard to believe, but even I have things that I want to keep private.'(Watson and Shakespeare, 2001)

Not only are these students aware of being treated differently but they also resent being seen and dealt with as a homo-geneous group rather than as individuals with different needs. There appears to be an assumption in some schools that they prefer the company of other disabled students. While bullying, taunts and teasing by able-bodied students is rife, they would like to be consulted about social preferences rather than having yet more decisions made for them about who they socialise with. This is complicated by the fact that the way space is organised in schools means that they are separated out and defined as a group during playtimes and lunchtimes, leading to a reinforcement of their sense of differentness. Even obvious signifiers like gender and race are eclipsed by their disability. It is not uncommon to find classes containing one girl and nine or more boys.

Based on the findings of this study, the researchers conclude:

> ...we have identified disabled children's ability to differentiate be-
> tween the adults they encounter in schools and to state why
> they prefer one adult over another. Disabled children are cap-
> able of identifying good practice. Our data suggests that where
> children encounter disablist practices in schools, they should be
> encouraged to put forward their own solutions to their problems.
> (Watson and Shakespeare, 2001)

Another study, this time a small scale survey of ten young
people with a range of physical and learning disabilities and
their families in Bolton, Lancashire (Whittles, 1998) sheds
different light on problems that they face in making their
views known. Within the formal mechanisms that exist in the
various local authority decision-making bodies, including a
joint consultative committee that has responsibility for children and young people, along with committees for education, etc., there was not a single representative from young
disabled people or their families. Neither was there a formal
process of consultation in order for their views to be heard.

As the report says:

> This seems to be a lost opportunity, as young disabled people
> and their parents are in a prime position to identify gaps in ser-
> vice provision, review how well service specifications and con-
> tracts are meeting their needs and help to evaluate the quality
> of services provided.

As well as strategic decision-making bodies not including or
consulting young people with disabilities, they are also
sometimes not invited to annual review or transition plan
meetings that directly affect them.

The composite picture that emerges is of these young people
being further disabled by being left out of the processes and
systems that affect their day to day lives, their longer term
plans and, in essence, their identity. As was found in the previous study, assumptions are made of their incapacity, of

their preferences, of their thoughts. They are not listened to and not heard.

Ethnic minorities

On the one hand, it is simplistic to talk about ethnic minority children's experience of school as if they are a homogeneous group. The ethnic minority population of Britain at the beginning of the 21st century is unprecedently diverse, representing all nations of the world, all social classes, languages, life experiences, religions and aspirations. And as such, they are widely divergent in their passage through the British education system. For instance, we know from the little data that exists that some groups, like Indians and Chinese, shine in British schools while others, particularly boys of African Caribbean descent, are more likely to be excluded and to achieve lower results than their peers.

We know from a London study (Richardson and Wood, 1999) of Key Stage 2 and GCSE results undertaken in the summer 1998 that:

- The achievement of African Caribbean pupils at KS2 was well below the national averge in most of the LEAs, with maths attainment particularly low.

- African Caribbean pupils at KS2 English was at the same level or higher than the national average in some authorities.

- At GCSE level throughout all the authorities, African Caribbean students' grades were considerably lower than the national level. In some of the LEAs, proportionally more than twice as many white students received five A*-Cs than their African Caribbean peers.

- Indian students achieve significantly higher than all other groups at both KS2 and GCSE. In some parts of London, Pakistani children achieve at or above the national average.

- In most of the 20 LEAs analysed, Bangladeshi children did less well than their white peers but higher than African Caribbean students.

We also know that ethnic minority families and schools often have problems understanding each other, feeling comfortable with each other, trusting each other.

The London study contains some revealing vignettes of pupils, parents, teachers and others that create an unsettling picture of divisiveness based on a lack of communication and mutual understanding. The following is an example.

> Last week we had an assembly on Martin Luther King's birthday. A school governor who was present commented afterwards: 'This is Britain, don't you think you should be teaching the children to be British? And what about our own English children? They're losing their identity, they don't know who they are, they have nothing to be proud of.' I didn't have a chance to reply. This week the governor has a letter in the local press saying the same things. (Richardson and Wood, 1999)

Another tells of a confrontation between an Ofsted inspector and a black teacher:

> An Ofsted inspector visiting the school the other day said the biggest problem facing British education today is poor attainment among white working class boys. 'You could also say,' remarked a colleague, who incidentally is a black woman, 'that a major problem is the high level of racism, sexism and homophobia amongst such boys.' 'So you think political correctness is more important than raising standards?' said the inspector. 'I strongly advise you, young lady, to change your views.' (ibid.)

And this, from an education welfare officer:

> I had occasion this week to be in the staffroom at a local school. There was some discussion of the Stephen Lawrence inquiry. Suddenly someone said: 'These race relations do-gooders, they're off the wall, they have no idea what it's like being a

teacher these days. League tables, the National Curriculum and pupils who challenge, question, argue, flaunt their sexuality, flaunt their strength. I've had it up to here.' Silence. Everyone seemed to look in my direction to hear what I would say. (ibid.)

But perhaps the most chilling is the quote from a black student.

I'm a Year 9 student. This week I wrote a poem in English about slavery. 'It's well expressed,' said the teacher, who's white, 'but terribly extreme. You don't really feel like that, do you? 'Of course I do,' I said. 'We all do. I'm angry about what you people did to us and you're still doing it.' 'It wasn't me that did it,' snapped the teacher, raising her voice, 'and anyway, I don't like the way you're talking to me about this.' And that was that. What next?

While it's impossible to know the story behind that story, what is clear is that the deeply rooted pain that the student expressed in his poem was seen not as an opportunity for meaningful discussion from which the whole class could have benefited, but as a threatening challenge to authority. And among other things, it reflects the alienation that many ethnic minority students feel day in, day out.

In her book, Maud Blair (2001) astutely makes a case for looking beyond the obvious, at the myriad factors that work against children who are 'other.'

By placing the problems faced by black students in a broader social as well as historical perspective, we can avoid the reductionism that can result from a focus on racism alone in the experience of black students... By addressing more broadly the systems of exclusion within education generally and the way that schools as institutions conduct their business, we are more likely to see that the problems which confront black students are rooted in an interplay of social factors of which racism is only one, albeit the one which arouses the most emotion in black students and their families and communities and is probably also the most dangerous.

Her findings, based on interviews with black students in a range of secondary schools in England, led her to conclude that:

> they feel a great deal of confusion and rage about their schooling, their prospects and the way they are positioned in society. They are fully aware that education is necessary and important but they are demoralised by a school system which denies them recognition through the curriculum, undermines their sense of self, appears indifferent to their needs, makes learning meaningless and is so intent on controlling them that they find little to distinguish between schools and detention centres. (Blair, 2001)

While her conclusions are grim, Blair offers a number of constructive recommendations to not only end the disproportionate numbers of black children being excluded from school but to prepare them to take their place in the outside world. Among them:

- try to address the tensions and stresses that teachers suffer

- listen to the perspectives of both teachers and students and create a school environment that is responsive to their views and also their skills

- restructure schools to make them relevant to the cultures and requirements of students today

- include in initial teacher training components on diversity and teaching in multi-ethnic contexts, including the ability to recognise ethnic and racial underpinnings of social discourses and their impacts on particular groups of students and an understanding of the mechanics of racism

- monitor academic progress by gender and ethnicity, review the results and take measures to reverse underachievement

- create a school culture that provides guidance to students, offers them compassion when they have problems and is generally characterised by respectfulness and good relations between staff and students

- include students in important policy issues such as be-haviour policy

- include parents and the local community on issues such as anti-discrimination policies

Some of these recommendations are undoubtedly sweeping and radical. But Blair contends that without them, the status quo will remain and further generations of black and ethnic minority students will feel alienated from a system that appears either not to be speaking to them or else doing so through clenched teeth.

The disaffected

Arguably the most marginalized and voiceless of all con-sumers of the education service are those who are dis-engaged from school, having either left, been excluded or being at risk of doing one or the other.

The disaffected also present arguably the most complex issues for schools. Are there children who are uncontainable in conventional school structures? How much do those structures themselves create disaffection in the unresilient, emotionally burdened child?

If there are dilemmas posed by disaffected students, there is at least one certainty: nobody gains from exclusion. Schools and individual staff members may feel they have failed the individual by not having necessary resources and outside support at their disposal. Peers are unsettled when the person is there to disrupt and also when they are removed. But it's the fate of the excluded students themselves that is the issue. Those who are permanently expelled from secon-dary school often are hurtled into an ever-descending spiral of low self-esteem, despair and anti-social behaviour. Only one in six returns to mainstream education. Of those who do not, some attend Pupil Referral Units, often erratically, while others receive only minimal home tuition each week. A large proportion will become involved in criminal activity of one form or another. A Home Office report (Graham, J and Bowling, B., 1995) points to the strong connection between exclusion and offending: all of the 11 male young offenders in the study and five of the eight females had been permanently excluded from school.

In a study of young people who have been excluded (Pomeroy, 2000), their relationships with teachers is presented as the dominant theme. Of their dislikes, many mentioned the absence of traits that Peter Woods discussed a decade ago in a description of students' criteria of 'the good teacher' (Woods, 1990): treating students with respectfulness in order to earn respect in return, 'being human', being able to talk to students.

Drawing on what the young people identified as the factors contributing to their disaffection with school and on particular models of good practice in Behavioural Support Service Centres and mainstream schools, Pomeroy makes the following suggestions:

- that teachers demonstrate the value they place on young people through respectful behaviour towards them and by interacting with them on a personal level

- that schools introduce other positive relationships between students and adults by providing support workers to befriend young people and work with them on particular social and emotional issues such as anger management and self-esteem

- that teachers make time to listen to young people

- that a positive whole school ethos is created which is supportive of pupils who are on the edge

- that power relations within the school are analysed, with a view to involving students more in a range of decisions that impact on them either directly or indirectly

Common threads

A look at these disparate groups highlights two points. Firstly, they bring home just how marginalized these groups are within the education system. Already disadvantaged by society at large, their disadvantage follows them into school. They feel typecast as either low achievers, troublemakers or both. They feel that their views are not solicited or listened to, that they are not consulted about issues that directly affect them and that they are denied rights that are enjoyed by other students.

Then there is the mismatch, not to say yawning chasm, that exists between what children want from their school experiences and what they get. Equality, fairness, stimulation, compassion, an interest in them as individuals and a belief in their abilities to succeed are what they and all young people want from their educational experience. That they feel shortchanged from school, treated differently from others and not listened to is not only an indictment of their schools but a recipe for disaffection and social problems later in life.

Whether they are black British or newly arrived refugees, whether they have been excluded or have disabilities, these young people share a sense of otherness because of how they believe they are treated, possibly by the world at large but more specifically by their schools.

CHAPTER 6

Summary

This book has shown how schools are taking up the challenge of sharing rights and responsibilities with their students in diverse, creative and exciting ways. It has illustrated how these initiatives and approaches impact positively on children and young people, their schools, the people who work in them – and ultimately society in general.

Participation is about learning communication skills, the democratic process and how to take one's place as citizens – not only as adults but now as children and young people. Giving children the experience of being involved in decision-making and policy-making, in dialogue and planning, in speaking and being listened to, in growing in their own esteem and respecting others, in enjoying rights and honouring responsibilities – if this isn't education for citizenship today and tomorrow, what is?

I hope that the examples that have been laid out in these pages have shown how schools can put the theory of participation into practice in different ways that reap rewards. Power sharing isn't a blueprint for anarchy. Far from giving the green light to chaos in the corridors, it brings new, more carefully defined structures and regulations to replace the old ones. These structures have the advantage that, because of the participation of the students themselves in formulating and developing them, they are more likely to be complied with and respected than those that were imposed by staff without consulting students.

Schools that are committed to sharing power by opening up mechanisms and procedures are by definition intent on school improvement and that being so, are prepared to look critically at their own practice and ethos. The process of involving students requires an honest analysis of the way the system has worked so far. It is underpinned with the knowledge that there were problems that need addressing. By choosing to take on change, schools acknowledge that their ideological foundations require revisiting and revision. And with that focus comes clarity.

In other words, the democratisation of schools is a process that benefits everyone. It is the ultimate in the joined up thinking that New Labour has striven to achieve. This is how it works schematically:

> When students are listened to, they are more engaged with their school and with their learning.

> As a result they are better behaved and achievement is raised.

> As a result teachers are more respectful of students and more fulfilled in their jobs.

> As a result the ethos of the school is improved.

Put that way it looks simple and of course it is anything but. The challenges, as we have seen, are significant, not least of all because of the thought, time and energy that is required to develop the structures and practice that are right for the school. But there is no doubt in the minds of researchers, those who have undertaken the challenge and the students and their parents, that the process and the product are well worth working towards.

So, too, believe Save the Children and the staff of the London Borough of Newham, who joined together as partners in this book. While coming from very different starting points – Save the Children's advocacy of children's rights and Newham's provision of inclusive education – they share a common and determined commitment to participation.

To set the process of democratising schools underway, schools will find it helpful to:

- develop a charter for students' participation that clearly lays out how and to what extent it will involve students, provide feedback to them and involve them in decision-making

- routinely canvass the views of students to hear what improvements and changes they feel are needed

- establish monitoring systems to analyse race, gender and disability equity in terms of exclusions, suspensions, attainment, attendance

- set up democratically elected student councils which are held accountable and regularly communicate with the rest of the school on its proceedings

- provide training for student council representatives in the range of skills they will require

- provide training for teachers and school governors on children's rights and participation

- create structures that allow for non-elected students to be involved in committees, working groups, consultations and other activities

- ensure that education for citizenship is given status by embedding children's rights and active citizenship opportunities into the curriculum

- set up schemes and programmes that promote the involvement of students in their learning and support

- provide students with regular opportunities each week to express their views and be listened to, including via circle time, and providing training for teachers to deliver it effectively

- provide a means of ensuring that students are involved in developing school policies

- set up effective communication channels with parents and keep them apprised of student council and other activities

- ensure school governing bodies elicit and take account of the views of students on matters that affect them and that they are accountable to students

- develop a school disciplinary policy in collaboration with students

- evaluate the effectiveness of school councils and other participatory activities

References

Alderson, P. (1999) *Civil Rights in Schools Project Report* Hull: Economic and Social Research Council

Alderson, P. (2000) Children's Rights and School Councils, *Children and Society* 14 pp 121-134 London: John Wiley and Sons

Alderson, P. (2000) School Students' Views on School Councils and Daily Life at School in *Children and Society* 14 pp. 121-134 London: John Wiley and Sons

Birkett, D. (2001) The School We'd Like in Education *Guardian* London

Blair, M (2001) *Why Pick on Me? School Exclusion and Black Youth* Stoke on Trent: Trentham Books

Challenging Transitions (2000-2001) London: Joseph Rowntree Foundation

Children 5-16 Research Briefing: Civil Rights in Schools (1999) London: Economic and Social Research Council

Children's Consortium on Education (2002) *Children's and Young People's Participation in Schools: Briefing paper on the Education Bill* London: Children's Consortium on Education

Children and Young People's Unit (2001) *Learning to Listen, Core Principles for the Involvement of Children and Young People* London: Department for Education and Skills

Crick, B. (1998) *Education for Citizenship and the Teaching of Democracy in Schools: Final Report of the Advisory Group on Citizenship* London: QCA

Cruddas, L., Dawn, S., Freedman, E., Pierre-MacFarlane, G., Smith, J. (2001) *Girls' Voices: are they on the agenda?* London: Newham Education Authority

Cruddas, L. and Haddock, L. (2003) *Girls' Voices: supporting girls' learning and emotional development* Stoke on Trent: Trentham

Cutler, D. and Frost, R. (2001) *Taking the Initiative: promoting young people's involvement in public decision-making in the UK* London: Carnegie Young People Initiative

Davies, L. (1999) *School Councils and Pupil Exclusions* Centre for International Education and Research, University of Birmingham for School Councils UK

Davies, L. and Kirkpatrick, G. (2000) *The Euridem Project: a review of pupil democracy in Europe* London: Children's Rights Alliance for England, Calouste Gulbenkian Foundation, NSPCC

Department for Education (1989) *Discipline in Schools*: report of committee chaired by Lord Elton London: HMSO

Department for Education (1994) *Code of Practice on the Identification and Assessment of Special Educational Needs* London: HMSO

Department for Education and Skills (2001) *SEN Toolkit Section 4: 'Enabling Pupil Participation'* Nottinghamshire: DfES Publications

Department for Education and Skills (2001) *Special Educational Needs Code of Practice* London: DfES

Economic and Social Research Council Network Project: Consulting pupils about teaching and learning. www.consultingpupils.co.uk

Fielding, M. (2001) Beyond the rhetoric of student voice: new departures or new constraints in the transformation of 21st century schooling *Forum* 43 (2) pp. 100-109

Galloway, D., Armstrong, D., Tomlinson, S. (1994) *The Assessment of Special Educational Needs: whose problem?* London: Longman

Gersch, I. (1996) Listening to Children in Educational Contexts in Davie, R., Upton, G., Varma, V. *The Voice of the Child* London: Falmer Press

Graham, J. and Bowling, B. (1995) *Young People and Crime* London: Home Office

Harber, C. (ed.) (1995) *Developing Democratic Education* Education Now Books

Hannam, D. (2001) Unpublished reported commissioned by the DfES on student participation

Hannam, D. (2001) Pilot study to evaluate the impact of the student participation aspects of the citizenship order on standards of education in secondary schools: an unpublished report commissioned by the DfES

HAYS (Horn of Africa Youth Scheme) (1998) *Let's Spell It Out: peer research on the educational support needs of young refugees and asylum seekers living in Kensington and Chelsea* written in partnership and published by Save the Children, UK, London

Highfield Junior School (1997) *Changing Our School: promoting positive behaviour* London: Institute of Education and Highfield Junior School

Howe, S. (2001) A Change of Pace *Times Educational Supplement: Special Needs Curriculum Special* 4

International Journal of Children's Rights (1997) pp 279-297

Jelly, M., Fuller, A., Byers., R (2000) *Involving Pupils in Practice: promoting partnerships with pupils with special educational needs* London: David Fulton

Kerr, D., Lines, A., Blenkinsop, S., Schagen, S., (2002) *Citizenship and Education at Age 14: A summary of the international findings and preliminary results for England; the views of students, teachers and schools in 28 countries* Slough: National Foundation for Educational Research

Klein, R. (2001) *Citizens by Right: citizenship education in primary schools* Stoke on Trent UK and Sterling VA USA: Trentham Books and Save the Children UK

Osler, A. (1997) *Exclusion from School and Racial Equality: research report* London: Commission for Racial Equality

Parsons, C., Castle, F., Howlett, K., Worrall, J. (2000) quoted in *Experiencing Exclusion* by Eva Pomeroy, Trentham Books, Stoke on Trent

QCA (1998) *Education for Citizenship and the Teaching of Democracy in Schools: final report of the advisory group on citizenship* London: QCA

Richardson, R. and Wood, A. (1999) *Inclusive Schools, Inclusive Society: Role and Identity on the Agenda* Stoke on Trent: Trentham Books for ROTA

Rudduck, J. and Flutter, J. (2000) Pupil Participation and Pupil Perspective *Cambridge Journal of Education* 30 (1)

Rudduck, J. and Flutter, J. (2002) *Consulting young people in schools.* www.consultingpupils.co.uk

Save the Children UK (2001) *Education Briefing Paper on White Paper Schools: Achieving Success* London: Save the Children UK

Save the Children UK (2001) *A Survey of Students on Participation* London: Save the Children UK

Save the Children UK (2002) *Green Paper Schools: Building on Success: responses from children and young people* London: Save the Children UK

Schargel, F. and Smink, J. (2001) *Strategies to Help Solve Our School Dropout Problem* New York: Eye on Education

School Councils UK website: www.schoolcouncils.org

Taylor, M. and Johnson, R. (2002) *School Councils: their role in citizenship and personal and social education* London: National Foundation for Educational Research

UNICEF (2000) *Citizenship in 400 Schools: a baseline survey of curriculum and practice among 400 UK primary, middle and secondary schools in summer 2000* London: UK Committee for UNICEF

Wagg, S (1996) Don't Try to Understand Them: politics, childhood and the new educational market in Pilcher, J. and Wagg, S. (eds.) *Thatcher's*

Children: Politics, Childhood and Society in the 1980s and 1990s London: Falmer Press

Watson, N., Shakespeare, T. *et al* (2001) Life as a disabled child: a qualitative study of young people's experiences and perspectives. An unpublished report that is part of the ESRC research programme 'Children 5-16: Growing into the 21st Century'

Weatherill, B (1990) *Report on the Speaker's Commission on Citizenship* London: HMSO

Whittles, S. (1998) *Can You Hear Us? Including the views of disabled children and young people in decision-making* London: Bolton Metropolitan Services and Save the Children UK

Woods, P. (1990) *The Happiest Days? How pupils cope with school* London: Falmer Press